IAN MCGRATH

Shadows
of
Redemption

Shadows of Redemption

C. H. WALLER

GOSPEL FOLIO PRESS
P. O. Box 2041, Grand Rapids, MI 49501-2041
Available in the UK from JOHN RITCHIE LTD.
40 Beansburn, Kilmarnock, Scotland

Originally published in 1881 by Sampson Low and Co.

Copyright © 1999
Gospel Folio Press
All Rights Reserved

Published by Gospel Folio Press
P.O. Box 2041, Grand Rapids, MI 49501-2041

Gospel Folio Press ISBN 1-882701-51-8

Cover design by J. B. Nicholson, Jr.
Cover illustration Copyright © 1997 New Tribes Mission, Inc.
For information regarding New Tribe's *Firm Foundations* Bible Survey,
contact: NTM, Inc., 1000 E. 1st Street, Sanford, FL, 32771

Printed in the United States of America

A glory gilds the sacred page,
Majestic like the sun;
It gives a light to every age,
It gives, but borrows none.

—WILLIAM COWPER

CONTENTS

Publisher's Foreword ix
1. Once for All 11
2. Jesus Christ the Same 25
3. The Coming of Our Lord 37
4. Holy Places 47
5. Bearing the Curse 59
6. In All Points Tempted 71
7. In the Wilderness 81
8. The Third Temptation 93
9. Just and Having Salvation 105
10. Stranger in Jerusalem 117
11. Seen of Me Also 131
12. The Print of the Nails 141
13. Follow Me 153
Scripture Index 169

PUBLISHER'S FOREWORD

We count it an honor to reintroduce a classic from the pen of C. H. Waller. Rich with the imagery of the Hebrew Scriptures, this book invigorates our faith and inflames our devotion to Heaven's lovely Man, of whom these types and shadows speak.

Referring to another book by the same author, Charles Spurgeon wrote in *Sword and Trowel,* "Intense has been our enjoyment of the deep spiritual thought contained in this volume…This is no common book. Those who love solid Scriptural teaching, and deep fellowship with God, will revel in these…holy meditations: we felt that we had seldom met with more satisfying food for thought. We hope to meet this author again."

I could not have better described my response to the writings of Charles Waller. And for those of you that have already found deep enjoyment in other of his books, we offer you the opportunity to "meet this author again."

In the preface to his first edition of this present

volume, dated July, 1881, Prof. Waller explains his purpose:

> "The greater part of this book is directly concerned with the Person and work of our blessed Saviour Jesus Christ. It is an attempt to set Him forth in some fresh aspects to those who are already acquainted with Him."

You cannot think too highly of Christ nor speak too well of Him. In fact, words fail us when we attempt to even describe Him as He is. But C. H. Waller thinks we ought to try. Our prayer as we reissue these meditations: "Let the beauty of the Lord our God be upon us: and establish Thou the work of our hands upon us; yea, the work of our hands establish Thou it" (Ps. 90:17).

J. B. NICHOLSON, JR.
Grand Rapids, Michigan

CHAPTER ONE

ONCE FOR ALL

For every high priest is ordained to offer gifts and sacrifices: wherefore it is of necessity that this man have somewhat also to offer.
HEBREWS 8:3

The offering made by our Lord Jesus Christ as our High Priest has been made the subject of much controversy. The Bible asserts most distinctly that it is a finished offering: "This Man, after He had offered one sacrifice for sins forever, sat down on the right hand of God."

If we believe that He "sitteth at the right hand of God in the glory of the Father," we must hold that His offering is concluded; for, not until He had completed it, did He sit down. The language of the creed of all Christendom is decisive on this point. If Christ now sits at the right hand of God, His offering must be complete.

But I did not mention this fact for the sake of presenting it controversially. It appears to me that the offering of Christ, as distinct from His sacrifice, is the meeting-point of several very instructive lines of thought in the Old Testament; that there is a great deal more in it than the simple proposition that it is an offering long since finished and complete.

First of all, let me say that the offering of Christ, as distinct from His sacrifice, fulfills two great offerings of the Levitical law, besides some lesser things. Those two, in the language of the law of Moses, are the meal offering, and the sin offering of the great Day of Atonement. One of them is an offering of blood and life, the other an offering of man's labor, but without the sacrifice of life. Both these are fulfilled and included in the offering made by our High Priest. To show how these two offerings differ, let us first refer to the law.

The meal offering is described in Leviticus 2. The first verse gives the principle of it: "When any will offer a meat offering," literally, an *offering,* a present or gift, "unto the Lord, his offering shall be of fine flour; and he shall pour oil upon it, and put frankincense thereon." He shall then bring it to the priests, who take out of it one handful, including part of the fine flour and oil and all the frankincense, and burn it on the altar for a memorial, or, as we should say, a sample, of the whole. This memorial went up to God in the fire of the altar; the remainder was given to the priests.

The second chapter of Leviticus describes various forms of meal offering.

In the first instance, it is to be fine flour and oil mixed together, but not in any way cooked or prepared for food. In other instances the preparation of the meal offering for food is carried a step further before it is offered; it is baked in an oven, or prepared in a pan, and then presented. But in all cases alike the ingredients were fine flour and oil, and a portion was burnt on the altar. Leaven was never allowed to be mixed with it, and salt was always required. In one instance the fruits of the earth were offered, as parched corn in the ear, not made into flour, but with oil and frankincense upon it. But in all cases the substance of the meal offering is the same. It is bread-corn, the food appointed for fallen man to obtain by labor, when he was expelled from Paradise. In all cases, except one, it is bread-corn bruised and made into fine flour; in some cases it is prepared for food, in one case also broken, but it is always mingled with oil before it is offered; and the name which describes it (a meat offering in the Authorized Version), means, in the original language, simply an offering, a present or a gift.

The word which describes this offering in the Old Testament is one of the words found in that passage of Psalm 40 which speaks directly of the offering of Jesus Christ: "Wherefore when He cometh into the world, He saith, sacrifice and offering (meal offering) Thou wouldest not, but a body hast Thou prepared Me. In burnt offerings and sacrifices for sin Thou hast had no pleasure. Then said I, Lo, I come, in the volume of the book it is written of Me, to do Thy will, O God" (vv. 6-8).

The remark made on this passage in the Epistle to the Hebrews is, that when Christ speaks of offering and sacrifice as no longer acceptable, He then says, "Lo, I come to do Thy will, O God." And it is added, "by the which will we are sanctified through the offering (meal offering) of the body of Jesus Christ once for all."

It appears from this passage that the body of Christ takes the place of the meal offering in Leviticus. The presentation of His body to do the will of God is the real meal offering. His obedient labor in the bodily form of man is the gift which God accepted as the fulfillment of that type in the old law. But the word *offering* is used in the Epistle to the Hebrews in such a way as to convey to us an entirely different notion from this which it carries in Psalm 40. There it is associated with sacrifice, as the *minchahs* or meal offerings of the Levitical law were always required to accompany the burnt offerings. But here, in the further use made of it by the writer of this epistle, it is the actual offering made by the high priest. And so in our text, "Every high priest is ordained to offer gifts and sacrifices: wherefore it is of necessity that this man should have somewhat also to offer." It is an offering made, not by priests, like the ordinary meal offerings, but by the high priest himself, and this brings us upon entirely different ground.

The high priest in Israel had only one meal offering to make, and that was made on the day he was anointed. It was an offering of bread-corn bruised into fine flour, mingled with oil, and also prepared for food, and then broken into pieces; an offering to be wholly burnt, and not to be eaten; an offering not for man, but all for God. It is a curious and interesting reminder to us, that the body which God prepared for Christ was offered to Him as a body broken—offered to Him in a way in which it could not be offered to any human being. But this fact is not alluded to in the Epistle to the Hebrews. The only offering made by the high priest, which is mentioned here, is that which no one but the high priest could make, the offering made in the Holy of Holies once a year on the Day of Atonement; an offering of blood and incense which the high priest must present within the veil.

This was not a meal offering, but a sin offering of a very peculiar kind. Whenever God required a sin offering to be made for all the people together, as distinct from that which might be required for anyone of them by himself, He demanded that evidence of the death of the victim should be brought to Him in the form of blood, a portion of the blood of the slain; brought and presented in His own dwelling place. And on the Day of Atonement it must be brought not only into the tabernacle, but into the Holy of Holies within the veil.

The body of the victim must at the same time be taken outside the camp of Israel, and there burnt with fire in the sight of all men, clean and unclean alike. Lepers and unclean persons, as well as Gentiles, might have seen the sin offerings consumed outside the camp. That is, God's wrath against sin must be publicly displayed on earth, and the blood of the victim must be presented as evidence of his death in the inner sanctuary, in the presence of God.

Now, the one part of this type was fulfilled in our Lord's crucifixion; but the other could not be actually fulfilled until His ascension into heaven, when He as the true High Priest passed within the veil. It does not say in the Epistle to the Hebrews that He took His blood there with Him. But it says more precisely that "by His own blood He entered." And forasmuch as He came thither with the marks of nails and spear upon His Person, and remains there upon His throne, "a Lamb as it had been slain," He certainly fulfilled the law which demanded the evidence of death to be presented at the throne of Jehovah within the veil.

There is thus a double idea in the offering of Christ as our High Priest. First there is the offering of His labor, the labor of His life as a man among men, for God and men. That answers to the *minchah* or meal offering of the law.

It was an offering of fine flour mingled with oil, and crowned with frankincense—of labor inspired, guided by the Holy Spirit, and crowned with purity; begun, continued, and ended in God; so that He could say, "I have glorified Thee on the earth, I have finished the work which Thou gavest Me to do." And it was prepared for food and broken, as He gave His broken body for our food.

There is this first, and secondly there is the presentation of Himself bearing the marks of death upon His Person, the marks of the sin offering completed, marks inflicted upon His body when He, the true sin offering, "suffered without the gate."

The offering of the body of Jesus Christ once for all included both these offerings. It was the presentation of labor finished, and the proof that sin had been "put away …by the sacrifice of Himself." This gift, and this sacrifice did our great High Priest come to offer for us all.

There is, however, another important thing to be noticed in the word *offering,* as applied to our Lord in the Epistle to the Hebrews. The English word *offering* has two meanings. It may signify the thing which is offered, as in the Psalms—"sacrifice and offering," that is, meal offering, such as is offered by the law; or it may signify the presentation of that which is offered, as in Hebrews 10:10, "By the which will we are sanctified through the offering," the presentation, "of the body of Jesus Christ once for all." Now if this meaning of presentation—the presenting of the body of Jesus Christ once for all, is always intended in the Epistle to the Hebrews wherever the word is used, it is obviously of the utmost importance to the argument; as in chapter 10:14, "By one offering He hath perfected forever them that are sanctified."

If one offering there means not merely one offered thing, such as one body of Christ, but one offering or presentation of that body, a great controversy is closed. For a single presentation of which the effect is complete cannot possibly be twisted into a number of successive presentations, or one prolonged and renewed presentation, of the offered thing.

We may well ask, therefore, regarding this word *offering* in the Epistle to the Hebrews, how the case really stands. What are the actual facts? Does the word *offering* mean the gift or present which is brought before God and given, or the act of presenting it?

To this question the original languages of the Old and New Testament give no doubtful answer. It is perfectly clear that the offering, the *minchah* of the Law, and the *prosphora* of the Epistle, are both words of that kind which properly denote, not the thing, but that which is done with the thing; the giving rather than the gift. By usage, the words came to signify the gift as well as the giving, but the giving or presenting is the first and principal idea. This meaning will make the sense complete everywhere; the other will not.

It appears, then, that it is not a matter of indifference whether we speak of the "one sacrifice" or the "one offering" of Jesus Christ. It is not quite the same to say, "there remaineth no more sacrifice," and "there remaineth no more offering" for sin. One victim, and one slaying, and one suffering, and one presentation of Him who was slain and suffered, are taught by the Epistle; one and no more than one.

And yet it would not be quite true to say that there are no steps and stages in the offering of the body of Jesus Christ. There are four at least mentioned in this Epistle. There is a step towards it in His incarnation: "When He cometh into the world, He saith, Sacrifice and *minchah* Thou wouldest not, but a body hast Thou prepared Me"— a body in which to do the work that would make the *minchah* or offering to God. This is the first step.

There is, secondly, that offering which our Lord made for Himself not by reason of sin, but by reason of His infirmity, or rather of our infirmity which hung about Him like a chain, "in the days of His flesh, when He offered up prayers and supplications with strong crying and tears unto Him that was able to save Him from death, and was heard in that He feared." This offering was made in Gethsemane.

It is described in chapter 5 of this Epistle, where it answers to the offering which the high priest made "for himself, by reason of infirmity —infirmity that was sinful in all other high priests, but not in our sinless Lord. But this is not the last stage.

Like the offering which the high priest made for himself, it preceded that which was made for the people. The third stage of our Lord's offering is that which completed His sacrifice. "The blood of Christ, who through the Eternal Spirit offered Himself without spot to God," was shed on Calvary.

And when He "released" and "breathed out" and "delivered up," His spirit for us in death, a spotless sacrifice to His Father, the sacrifice was complete. Virtually the offering was complete also, for the "veil of the temple was rent in twain—from the top to the bottom," showing that no more need be done to give Him the right of entrance there.

We see, then, that at His incarnation when He came to do God's will, and in Gethsemane where He said—as it has never been said before or since—"Not My will, but Thine, be done," and again at His death, our Lord made an offering. But not one of these three nor all of them together can quite satisfy the words of our text, for this reason: those offerings were made on earth, and the very next verse reminds us, that "if He were on earth, He should not be a priest."

Our text requires that He should not only offer, but offer as a high priest, and this He can only do in heaven, because on earth He had no right to the priesthood. He never entered into the Holy of Holies in God's earthly temple. It remained, then, that He should present, or offer, the result of all this which He had done before the throne of God in heaven.

This He did at His ascension, when He entered "into heaven itself, now to appear in the presence of God for us," and there to present in His own person the evidence of all He had done and suffered here, the body which God had prepared for Him, and in which He had finished the work that God gave Him to do.

This presentation of Himself He made when He ascended, but not altogether like the Jewish high priests. For they came in stealthily as it were, passing round the two corners of the double veil. They hid themselves behind a cloud of smoking incense, lest the glory should burst upon them and they should die. And then after a few moments they retired, having left the blood behind them which they came to sprinkle, and they returned again the next year to repeat their work.

But our High Priest entered gloriously, not to hide Himself, but "to appear." And He did not retire after He had entered, nor did He remain standing before the mercy seat, but took His seat upon the midst of the throne, and there He is unto this day—not a priest standing before an altar, but "a priest upon His throne." "For He must reign, til [God] hath put all enemies under His feet." He "sitteth at the right hand of God in the glory of the Father."

Now this contrast between Him and the high priests of Israel is hinted at in the words of our text. The word "offer" occurs twice in it. "Every high priest is ordained to offer gifts and sacrifices wherefore it is of necessity that this man should have somewhat also to offer." There is no difference in the English. But in the original there is, and the difference may be thus expressed. "Every high priest is ordained to be offering gifts and sacrifices, wherefore it is of necessity that this man should have something which he may offer," that he may offer at one time; one offering which he may make.

When, therefore, our text is cited, as it is habitually by a well-known writer, to prove the offering of our Lord to be continuous, a very unpleasant alternative presents itself, which I hardly like to state, and yet do not see how I can honestly avoid. Either that writer is aware of the difference in the original, or he is not. If he is, why does he never refer to it? If he is not, does he really know enough of the matter to be a trustworthy guide?

And not in our text only, but throughout the whole Epistle, wherever the offering of Christ is mentioned, it is treated as a single act. Everyone who can read the Greek Testament can judge this for himself. In one place, indeed, the continuous offering is denied with regard to our Lord, "Nor yet that He should offer Himself often, as the high priest...for this He did once for all when He offered up Himself" (Heb. 9:25).

The final presentation of our Lord's work and person is therefore a presentation made in heaven, and it is a single presentation, a complete presentation, which is followed by His ascension to His Father's throne. To point out the contrast, we may say that it is the same thing exactly as if the high priest had first offered the blood in the Holy of Holies, and had then sat down upon the mercy-seat between the golden cherubim, above the ark of God. Which of all Aaron's posterity could have dreamed of acting so?

And if it be asked, in view of all this, what are we to think of our Lord's intercession, let me say that intercession is quite as effectual from the throne as from the altar. If one of us wishes to obtain a favor from some person who is above our own rank in this world, who is the best medium to employ? Obviously, the friend we have who happens to be nearest in rank to the person with whom he intercedes. If I were to desire promotion from the Queen or her chief minister, and I have a personal friend who is a member of the government, clearly he is the friend I need. So, in the relations between God and us, who is the best intercessor? Surely the Friend we have who is nearest in rank to God. There is none better than the Lord Jesus, for who can be nearer to man than He who is the Son of Man? And who can be nearer to God than He is, who is "very God of very God"? And there is no need to set Him before an altar. Indeed, we cannot if we would. Both the altars in God's house were outside the veil. The high priest is within. He must pass the altar before he could go in there. There is no altar in the Holy of Holies.

Which would you rather trust? Which is the most likely to prevail for you, the priest outside the veil before the altar, or the Priest within the veil upon the throne? Can there be a doubt about it? Surely there can be none. And although the one offering is effectual forever until the day of grace is over; and as long as the ark, the throne of the Lord, stands in the midst of Jordan, the tide of death cannot pass it, but Jordan is driven back; yet surely

ONCE FOR ALL

the offering is accepted once for all. And when a present is accepted you cannot present it over again. Let the presentation be as grand as you will, it cannot possibly go on forever, unless the present is refused.

How long is He who presents the gift to stand waiting for its reception? Will God the Father keep His dear Son Jesus Christ standing before His throne, as men keep Him standing at the door of their hearts, always knocking and never getting in? To refuse a gift is an insult. The longer it is presented without being accepted, the less likely is it to prevail.

Think not that our High Priest is treated so in heaven. Surely, if we do think so, God might justly answer us, "Thou thoughtest that I was altogether such an one as thyself: but I will reprove thee, and set them in order before thine eyes" (Ps. 50:21).

To conclude, what better lesson can we draw from this text for ourselves than this? If God has accepted His dear Son Jesus Christ and admitted Him to a throne in heaven, let us not keep Him waiting for entrance into our hearts on earth. He did not need to knock long at the gate of heaven. The gates lifted up their heads. The everlasting doors were lifted up, and the veil opened wide for the King of Glory to come in.

Why should we delay to admit Him here? "Behold," He says, "Behold, I stand at the door (the door of your hearts) and knock. If any man hear My voice and open the door, I will come in to him, and will sup with him, and he with Me. He that hath an ear, let him hear what the Spirit saith unto the churches" (Rev. 3:20, 22).

CHAPTER TWO

JESUS CHRIST THE SAME

*Jesus Christ the same yesterday,
and today, and for ever.*
Hebrews 13:8

What is a Christian's year except a record of the acts of the Lord Jesus for us men and for our salvation? His coming in great humility, first to His own people, yet manifested to the Gentiles as their King. His circumcision, fasting and temptation, His precious death and burial, His glorious resurrection and ascension and the coming of His Holy Spirit. All these things come before us. What time it is with us, that time it is as regards Him. Now our attention is to be directed to His coming, His second coming and also His first. The facts are the same still. But the glory of the person whom they concern is infinite.

"Yesterday, today and for ever," He must far exceed all that we can say or think or find out about Him.

There is only one sense in which it can be said to a person's honor and credit that he is the same yesterday and today and for ever. If it means that there is nothing fresh about him, nothing more to be learned from him, no improvement or progress in him, nothing more to be known about him, then to sum up his character in these words would suggest mere weariness and dreariness. But this, I need hardly say, is not the thought in the text.

It is in His relation to us that Jesus Christ is the same. He does not change in His faithfulness. And in the way of salvation He is the same. To be an unchanging friend, the same yesterday and today and for ever in that relation, is one of the most honorable things that can be said of anyone. And I think we can prove from the context that this was the thought in the writer's mind when he penned this most beautiful expression, "Jesus Christ the same yesterday, and today, and for ever."

The text stands between two different exhortations, one relating to persons and the other to doctrines. Our English Bible connects it with the verse before. Other editions connect it with what follows. As a matter of grammar, it stands by itself, and is not immediately connected with either. In thought it makes a beautiful resting-place between the two. Let us read it first with what goes before, " Remember," he says, "remember them which have the rule over you" (or rather your leaders), "who have spoken unto you the Word of God; whose faith follow, considering the end of their conversation," the issue of their lives, the closing scene of their Christian walk and converse here below. Remember how their walk ended, in short, how they died.

To what names in particular he refers we cannot tell.

JESUS CHRIST THE SAME

They may be in part the names of martyrs, like Stephen, and James the brother of John, and James the Lord's brother. I cannot say that these very names are intended, because it is by no means clear to me that the Epistle was written to Jerusalem. But if it was, these saints may have been in the writer's mind. Certainly the persons to be remembered are some who have departed hence in the fear of God and in the faith of Christ. The word "end" proves it; for there can be no question that "the end of their conversation" means the closing scene of their lives. And, in that view, what a wealth of meaning the words have gained as years have rolled by. "Some are fallen asleep" was all that could be said of the church of Christ then. The greater number of them were on earth. Now, they who are fallen asleep in Christ are the majority. How many triumphant deaths are included in that expression "the end of their conversation!" Who is there that cannot recall some? This is the introduction to our text, and a very beautiful introduction it is.

Some of these triumphant deaths and closing scenes, though "joy unspeakable and full of glory" to those who departed to be with Christ, have been unspeakable sorrow to those who were left behind. As the death of John the Baptist abruptly interrupted and suspended the first mission of the twelve apostles in the lifetime of our Lord, so with the deaths of others that have befallen since. The whole face of the church's heaven has seemed to be overcast with the cloud that withdrew some revered and beloved member from the sight of the rest.

And as on the death of John the Baptist they left off

everything else and "went and told Jesus," so it has been since. When all other shepherds depart, He, the Chief Shepherd, remains, "Jesus Christ the same yesterday, and today, and for ever." That I think is the latent thought that connects our text with what goes before. Remember those that have been leaders and have gone away. But above all remember Him who never goes away; who said, "Lo, I am with you alway, even to the end of the world."

This is the "setting" of the text on the one side; and on the other it is quite as plain. If He of whom all doctrine speaks is the same, why change the doctrines? "Be not carried about with divers and strange doctrines." If you have known Him at all, be sure He has not altered. Then do not think it necessary to alter your thoughts of Him. And if I might venture to make a suggestion here as to the completion of this glorious text, it would be that it means this: not simply that Jesus Christ is the same; but let Jesus Christ be the same, yesterday and today and for ever. That He is the same is a fact that goes without saying. Then let Him be the same to you.

I should like just to point out the reason for taking the words thus, as it may not be obvious to a reader of the English Bible. The text stands in the midst of a number of precepts and instructions from verse 1, "Let brotherly love continue." "Be not forgetful to entertain strangers." "Remember them that are in bonds as bound with them." "Let marriage be had in honor in all respects and let the bed be undefiled, for (not but) fornicators and adulterers God will judge." Again, "Let your conversation be without covetousness; and be content with such things as ye have: for He hath said, I will never leave thee, nor forsake thee." "Remember them which have the rule over you, who have spoken unto you the Word of God: whose faith follow, considering the end of their conversation." Then our text, and again, verse 9, "Be not carried about with divers and strange doctrines" again, verse 16, "To do good and communicate forget not," and again, verse 17, "Obey them that have the rule over you," and again, verse 18, "Pray for us." Thus all is precept and exhortation down to the benediction in verse 20.

I think this verse is meant to be taken like the others. The grammatical construction is the same with verses 4 and 5. Jesus Christ was the sum and substance of Paul's teaching. He had two great subjects of discourse. One, what the Old Testament said, that the Christ should be a suffering, risen Christ; another, that Jesus was the Christ. In this Epistle, which is Paul's doctrine (whatever it is not), you have many things about the Christ and many about Jesus, and there is something special about every place that mentions the name of Jesus in this Epistle, from the first to the last. Here the two are united, Jesus Christ, not Christ only. Not only King, Messiah, the Hope of Israel, but Jesus Christ, Jesus of Nazareth, the King of the Jews, Christ crucified; Jesus Christ, and no other Christ. Let Jesus be your Christ, "the same yesterday, and today, and for ever." Let nothing alter your minds about Him. Let nothing darken your view of Him; but "let us run with patience the race set before us," looking fixedly unto Him.

Let us now consider for a few moments what is

SHADOWS OF REDEMPTION

implied in this statement that He is (and is to be to us) "the same yesterday, and today, and for ever," and what was "yesterday" in the mind of the writer of the Epistle, and what was known "yesterday" of Jesus Christ. When this Epistle was written, it was but early morning in the history of the Church of Christ. Yesterday all was Judaism. Yesterday the double name, Jesus Christ, was not put together. He who today is Jesus Christ was yesterday "the Angel of the Covenant;" as it is written: "The Lord whom ye seek, shall suddenly come to His temple, even the messenger (or Angel) of the Covenant, whom ye delight in: behold he shall come, saith the Lord of Hosts."

These words may serve to remind us of what we know perfectly well, but do not always realize: that He who lived on earth as Jesus of Nazareth was the same who had come to Israel as the Angel of Jehovah many a time before. He had been the Shepherd of Israel for many centuries before He came to lay down His life for the lost sheep. And one way of seeing that He is the same yesterday and today is to recall what we have read of Him in the Old Testament as the Angel of Jehovah, and to notice the likeness between what He said and did then as an Angel, and what He said and did afterwards as the Son of Man.

I need hardly stop to prove that the Angel of Jehovah and Jesus Christ are the same person in different natures. But if proof is required, take it in the words of John 1:18 "No man hath seen God at any time; the only begotten Son (or as some read, God only begotten) which is in the bosom of the Father, He hath declared Him."

Whenever God showed His face to men it was His

Son that they saw. In the first place in the Old Testament where the Angel of Jehovah is named, we find Him seeking a lost sheep of the house of Abraham. That lost sheep was Hagar, the mother (in-law she may be called) of all that are cast out and lost, and "The Angel of the Lord found her by a fountain of water in the wilderness, by the fountain in the way to Shur" (Gen. 16:7).

How came He to find her? What brought Him to that fountain in the wilderness? Did He want water, think you? Did He say, "Give Me to drink," as He said to another lost sheep at the well of Sychar? No; yesterday and today He had meat to eat and water to drink that men knew not of. In His Father's house there was enough and to spare. "For with Thee is the fountain of life." It was not want of any kind on His part that brought Him there. No, but the Angel of Jehovah yesterday, like the Son of Man today, had come "to seek that which was lost, until He found it." He sought it in the strength of His immortality, as the Angel of Jehovah. He sought it still in the weariness of His journey as the Son of Man.

Yesterday and today He is the anointed Saviour, "Jesus Christ the same yesterday and today." Yes, and not today only; He has not forsaken His calling as a Shepherd yet. In the world to come, they that are gathered into His fold "shall hunger no more, neither thirst any more, neither shall the sun light on them, nor any heat." Why not? Because "the Lamb which is in the midst of the throne shall be their Shepherd, and shall lead them unto living fountains of waters, and God shall wipe away all tears from their eyes."

SHADOWS OF REDEMPTION

In connection with the seeking after the lost, there is one mention of the Angel of Jehovah that seems to me very remarkable. I allude to the time when He came to preach repentance to Israel after the death of Joshua, when they were beginning to forsake His holy ways. The Angel of Jehovah went up from Gilgal to Bochim, went up from place to place through the country, remonstrating with the people as He went, or else gathering them together to hear His word, and most touching were the words He spake, "I made you to go up out of Egypt and have brought you unto the land which I sware unto your fathers, and I said, I will never break My covenant with you." In other words, I am the same today that I was yesterday, and I have promised to be the same to you for ever; but you, you have been unfaithful. "Why have you done this?"

Who can wonder that the people on hearing His remonstrance "lifted up their voice and wept"? Even so, a few words or a look from the Lord Jesus upon earth would melt a sinner's heart, or the heart of a backslider, to come in and stand at His feet weeping, or to go forth and weep bitterly outside. It was the same speaker, yesterday and today: "never man spake like this man." What will it be to live within hearing of that voice for ever, not on earth but in heaven?

But if He was so good to the lost when He sought them, what was He to His own sheep whom He had found?

Hear Jacob's testimony. It was "the God that was my Shepherd all my life long unto this day, the Angel which redeemed me from all evil" (see Gen. 48:15-16).

Remember how He came and visited Abraham, and sat at his tent door and ate with him, and told him what he was about to do, and heard his intercession for Sodom to the very end. Remember how He talked to Moses face to face, how He showed him His glory and accompanied him to the last hour of his life; how He wrestled with Jacob all the night and blessed him in the morning; how His own hands ministered to his weary servant Elijah, preparing his food while he slumbered, and waking him with His own gentle touch to eat and drink. Is it not the same who came at night to His toiling disciples, walking on the sea; and again in the morning, after they had toiled all night and taken nothing, giving them the miraculous supply of food? Yes, and again after the resurrection, calling them to the land where the fire and food were ready which no human hands had prepared.

As He drew out Jacob's faith at Peniel by first withholding and apparently refusing what He meant to give, so He drew out the faith of the Syrophenician woman, until they said, each in their own way, "I will not let Thee go, except Thou bless me." As He came to the toiling disciples on the sea, so He had walked with three faithful men in the midst of the fiery furnace; yes, and sat with Daniel in the lions' den. As He noticed Gideon threshing wheat by the winepress, and threshing like a mighty man of valor too, so He observed Matthew the publican sitting at the receipt of custom and said to both alike, "Follow Me."

Also note how He liked to conceal Himself and talk

awhile to men before they discovered Him. So He did to Gideon and Manoah in the Old Testament. So did He to two disciples on the first Easter Day. What wonder that the last Old Testament prophet should call Him "the Angel of the Covenant whom ye delight in," and the first prophet of the New Testament should "rejoice greatly because of the Bridegroom's voice"?

I have but touched lightly on a few particulars, but it is a line of thought which every reader of the Bible may easily improve. Only read those wonderful stories of the appearance of Jehovah as the Angel in the Old Testament, and say to yourself, "It was Jesus Christ, the same yesterday and today, the same Good Shepherd to sinful men." Look at Him, and see if you cannot recognize Him, and learn what He was like. The longer you look, the more you will discover of His beauty, who is "fairer than the children of men." Yes, and your own eyes will desire "to see the King in His beauty," and to behold Him in "the land that is very far off."

We might, if we desired, find the sterner side of His nature also in His opposition to Israel's foes. The Angel of Jehovah has been seen with a sword drawn in His hand also; drawn once against Jerusalem, more than once against those who would have injured His own sheep. But I do not desire to dwell now on this part of His character.

For proof that He is the same still, compare some of His words spoken from heaven to His servant John the beloved disciple, and through him to all the churches. We have seen Him seeking the lost and proclaiming repentance, as the Angel of the Covenant and as the Son of

Man. The epistles to the seven churches clearly show that He has not ceased to preach it from heaven, while the day of grace lasts.

There is one particular expression that I often wonder at, in His words to the lukewarm church of Laodicea. To that church He said, "As many as I love, I rebuke and chasten; be zealous therefore and repent." That word "I love" is never found on the lips of our Saviour to express His own affection to any others except to these. It is the word that He let Peter win from Him as it were with difficulty when "He saith unto him the third time…Lovest thou me?" And there it is "Lovest thou," not "I love." Peter had used it twice already before the Lord used it at all (of course I take the words which we have in the original New Testament as representing most accurately what was said, in whatever language it may have been spoken then). But here, unsolicited, unsuggested by the church that loved nothing dearly except itself—to the church to whom He had spoken words of loathing, "because thou art lukewarm and neither cold nor hot." He says at last, "As many as I dearly love I rebuke and chasten." It is a perfect example of "overcoming evil with good," thus to lavish the warmth of His own affectionate nature upon those who had not yet learned to love. I must not prolong the discourse upon this subject, wonderful and inexhaustible as it is.

We are treading on holy ground when we draw nigh to inspect His personal character. I have ventured thus to speak. May He forgive what has been spoken amiss by unclean lips concerning His glory! But let us never dishonor His faithfulness, or slight His offered love. Let Jesus Christ be the same to us, or rather let Him be more to us today than yesterday, and let us try to be something more to Him, for He is enough to be our portion forever.

If we have left our first love, let Him call us back to it. If His image has grown dim in our memories, the Holy Spirit can brighten it. It is His office to glorify Jesus Christ "to receive of His" (and what is there that is not His?) "and to show it unto us." Let Him then be the same to us, or in other words, let us "abide in Him," and thus prepare for His advent, which every return of the season brings nearer; and no one can tell how near it is. "And now, little children, abide in Him, that when He shall appear we may have confidence, and not be ashamed before Him at His coming."

CHAPTER THREE

THE COMING OF OUR LORD

*Be patient therefore, brethren,
unto the coming of the Lord.*
JAMES 5:7

We all recall, more or less, what we have been taught to expect as the fulfillment of prophecy. The things which have been written aforetime are sure to come to pass. And all readers of the Bible have some expectations, more or less definite, as regards the future. There are prophecies to be fulfilled that concern the Jews, God's ancient people. There are prophecies to be fulfilled that concern the Gentiles, the nations and kingdoms of the world. And there are also prophecies awaiting fulfillment that concern the church. All these prophecies form a part of the many things that were "written aforetime…for our learning, that we through patience and comfort of the Scriptures might have hope."

Now it makes considerable difference to our thoughts and views regarding the fulfillment of prophecy whether we are looking out for the coming of certain events and the accomplishment of certain predictions, or for the coming of a certain Person. One of these is very much more impressed and urged upon us in the Bible than the other. And can there be any question which of the two is most dwelt upon? Is it not clear that, if we are called on to look at the progress of events at all, it is for the sake of the Person whose coming they portend? "When these things begin to come to pass, then look up, and lift up your heads; for your redemption draweth nigh." Your redemption, in other words, your Redeemer. No one who reads or thinks about these things at all in the present day can fail to be struck with the exceeding rapidity with which events develop in the time in which we live. Almost before a thing is contemplated as possible, we see it done before our eyes.

Now we all ought to bring our minds to contemplate the possibility of the coming of our Lord Himself in our own lifetime. It cannot well be long delayed, though no man knows the day nor the hour. And there is nothing, so far as I know, in the whole course of prophecy to prevent its taking us by surprise at any moment. Take us by surprise it must, come when it will. The more need to be always ready. And I want to point out to you that the principal things foretold, for the Jews, for the Gentiles, and for the church of God, in prophecy, are each of them to be accomplished by the personal coming of our Lord.

First, the conversion of the Jews. I refer to Romans 11:25-26: "For I would not, brethren, that ye should be ignorant of this mystery, lest ye should be wise in your own conceits; that blindness in part is happened to Israel, until the fullness of the Gentiles be come in. And so all Israel shall be saved: as it is written, There shall come out of Zion the Deliverer, and shall turn away ungodliness from Jacob."

Of the restoration and conversion of Israel this chapter leaves no doubt at all. If Gentiles here mean Gentiles, Israel must mean the Jews. No one questions the meaning of the term Gentile. We cannot, therefore, question, that the meaning of the opposite name, Israel, is just as plain. The Jews then are to be converted. But how and by whom? By Christ Himself at His second coming, as it is written: "There shall come out of Zion the Deliverer, and shall turn away ungodliness from Jacob."

And it is not some kind of spiritual coming that is here intended. It is the personal appearance of Christ Himself. As the turning point in the history of Jacob's family, the immediate cause of their reunion was the personal reconciliation of Joseph and his brethren, when "at the second time" (as Stephen reminds us) he was made known to them, so it is to be hereafter. When He last left their temple, He departed with these solemn words: "Behold, your house is left unto you desolate. For I say unto you, ye shall not see Me henceforth, till ye shall say, Blessed is He that cometh in the name of the Lord." Three days after He said those words, He was crucified. He never entered their temple again. Until they welcome His coming, He and they remain apart.

We cannot say, therefore, that Christ is not to be expected until we have seen the restoration of the Jews *en masse*. Rather, the conversion of the nation cannot be expected until the personal appearing of the Lord Jesus. And until they are converted, it is only in a very limited sense that they can be restored.

Next, as to the Gentiles, the great thing the Gentile world has to look forward to is the subjugation of all earthly kingdoms to the kingdom of Christ. This event cannot take place till His second coming. We read in Daniel 2:44, in the vision, that the kingdom of the God of heaven shall "break in pieces and consume all the kingdoms" of the earth, strong or weak, whether they inherit the nature of the iron, the clay, the brass, silver, or gold. Whatever be the form of government, or the nature of the constitution, all alike are to be swept away together, and the kingdom of the God of heaven is to take their place.

What is the figure selected to represent that kingdom? It is a stone cut out of a mountain, or rather out of the Rock, without hands. It "smote the image upon his feet" and crushed it utterly to dust, with one and the same blow pulverizing the whole statue and blowing the dust of it away. And what is the stone? Christ Himself says two things concerning it in Matthew 21: "Did ye never read in the Scriptures: The stone which the builders rejected, the same is become the head of the corner." "And whosoever shall fall on this stone shall be broken: but on whomsoever it shall fall, it will grind him to powder."

Peter in the Acts says that the stone is Christ Himself (Acts 4:10-12). "Jesus Christ of Nazareth, whom ye crucified, whom God raised from the dead…This is the stone that was set at nought of you builders." Thus we see who and what it is that will remove the kingdoms of this world. It is no other than Christ Himself. Not His doctrine, not His gospel, not His law, not His ministers, not His church, but He Himself, that stone. He shall crush and winnow away all Gentile kingdoms and take their place. "The stone that smote the image" will "become a great mountain and fill the whole earth." The kingdoms of this world shall become the kingdoms of our Lord and of His Christ, and "He shall reign forever and ever." And His members shall reign with Him. Thus the great things foretold in Holy Scripture regarding Jew and Gentile are to be done by Christ Himself.

It is no less true concerning that to which the church looks forward. Take that parable in Luke 18, the parable that is nearest of all gospel parables to the precept in our text.

He spake a parable unto them to this end, that men ought always to pray, and not to faint; saying, There was in a city a judge, which feared not God, neither regarded man: and there was a widow in that city; and she came unto him, saying, Avenge me of mine adversary. And he would not for a while: but afterward he said within himself, Though I fear not God, nor regard man; Yet because this widow troubleth me, I will avenge her, lest by her continual coming she weary me. And the Lord said, Hear what the unjust judge saith. And shall not God avenge His own elect, which cry day and night unto Him, though He bear long with them? I tell you that He will avenge them speedily. Nevertheless when the Son of man cometh, shall He find faith on the earth?

The widow in this parable answers to God's elect. The unjust judge at last avenged the poor widow, because of her importunity. Shall not God avenge His own elect? The parable therefore refers specially to the true believers in Christ, not the visible church in its outward organization, but His own elect, the true Christians within the church, the very sheep of Christ, whom He knows and who are known of Him.

Now, what is it that He sets before them in this parable as their prospect on earth? It is not exactly a bright prospect as regards this world, but rather the reverse. They are likely to find themselves in the situation of that poor widow, who came again and again to the judge with the same petition: "Avenge me of mine adversary." The grievances are not told exactly. They are partly temporal, partly spiritual; but they will be such as must lead them to cry day and night unto God. And they will be grievances of which there appears to be no redress here on earth. I say no redress on earth, because of the last sentence. "When the Son of Man cometh, shall He find the faith on the earth?"

I cannot agree with those who understand "the faith" in this verse to mean Christianity. There is no proof whatever of the use of the phrase in this sense before the Acts of the Apostles. In that book we do read of "the faith," meaning "the faith of Christ." But at the time when our Lord spoke, Christianity as a separate faith had no existence. It was true Judaism—the belief in a Messiah promised, and the personal acknowledgment of Him who then lived and walked as a Jew among Jews.

THE COMING OF OUR LORD

Besides, if Christianity were to disappear from the earth before our Lord's second coming, who would there be to meet Him? What elect would there be to avenge? That cannot be the meaning of the text. Rather let us take it as simply as possible. "Shall not God avenge His own elect who cry day and night unto Him, though He bear long with them? I tell you that He will avenge them speedily. Nevertheless, when the Son of Man cometh, will He find the belief (of this fact) upon the earth?" The form of this question expects the answer, No. He will not find it. Why not?

The reasons are plain on the face of the parable. Did the widow expect the judge to avenge her? Not in the least. She had become so used to coming to him, and to his taking no notice, that it is hard to say why she came at all, except that the oppression of her adversary was unbearable, and she had no one else to go to. Did her adversary expect the judge's hand to be laid upon him? Not he. He felt secure in the long enjoyment of his neighbor's gains. That which he had taken from the poor widow, he had for some time regarded as his own. He had ceased to trouble himself about her, or to fear the effect of her applications to the unjust judge.

No two persons in that city were more surprised than the poor widow and her adversary, when the unjust did justice for once in his life. This parable has had more than one illustration in the history of the church of God since. In the time of the apostles, when Jewish persecution made the state of Christians almost unbearable, who could have thought of the sudden downfall of Jerusalem, which was to them the intervention of Christ? Or, after the tenth great Roman persecution, when the Christians were in utter despair, who would have expected such a change as the sudden conversion of the whole Roman empire, and the establishment of Christianity as the religion of the state? "When the Lord turned again the captivity of Zion, we were like them that dream. Then was our mouth filled with laughter, and our tongue with singing."

But neither of these things, though they illustrate the parable, can be said to have fulfilled it. It belongs in its final application to the coming of the Son of Man. And when He comes, we have a hint that the state of things in which He will find His elect will be that of the poor widow, crying out for deliverance from the adversary, deliverance which there is not the remotest earthly prospect of being able to obtain. The adversary will not believe it. His elect will have ceased to look for it, but go on crying, almost as it were mechanically, because there is no other refuge. It is not a bright prospect, but it drives us to one refuge, and one only, the coming of the Lord Himself. Perhaps to some of us the language of this parable may appear wholly unlike the state of things in which we live. We for the present are able to serve God in peace and safety, and what adversary is there to fear? It is so, thank God, with ourselves at this moment. It is not so even now with all who are near and dear to us, and we are not living in very settled times. And I may fairly ask the question, whether, in the days in which we live, simple justice is a thing easily obtained. Never was more noise and outcry made about injustice and wrongdoing. But when the noise is made, what is done? Chiefly nothing. Is it not very nearly true that those who can make themselves heard by reason of their clamorous importunity, obtain what they desire, be it what it may, and the rest may take their chance? Now, if that is the state of things—and it is not very far from that, I am sure—you have one more point of resemblance between the present times and that parable. And this brings us to the point of the instruction in the text.

"Be patient therefore, brethren, unto the coming of the Lord." When the Son of Man cometh, then and not till then, will His own elect be avenged. That is the thing for His church to look forward to. That will calm the world. That will restore His people.

"This Man shall be the peace." "He is just and having salvation." He Himself, and no one else. And the parable to which I have referred in Luke gives the law of patience. It was spoken "to the end that men ought always to pray and not to faint." Even if prayers appear to have no practical effect on the state of things in this world, on the ills we desire to remedy, they have effect somewhere. They "entered into the ears of the Lord of Sabaoth." "Shall not God avenge His own elect, which cry day and night unto Him?" Let us learn to pray more incessantly, and let us study this in our prayers, that they are so made as to reach Him to whom we speak. For, if we know that He hear us, we know that all is well. He never forgets. He never slumbers. All will be remembered and answered at the coming of the Lord.

CHAPTER FOUR

HOLY PLACES

For we have heard him say, that this Jesus of Nazareth shall destroy this place, and shall change the customs which Moses delivered us.
Acts 6:14

This text is part of the accusation brought against Stephen by his opponents, and supported by false witnesses. The charge, in the sense in which they made it, was false; and, whatever Stephen may have said on the subject in question, he had said nothing that would have brought him fairly within the grasp of the law. Yet we know that in some sense the words were true. For not many years afterwards, "Jesus of Nazareth" did actually "destroy this place" and utterly abolished many of the customs which He had Himself delivered to Moses for the children of Israel to observe.

Further, it was no more than our Lord Himself had foretold. Concerning the temple as a material building, He had said, "There shall not be left here one stone upon another that shall not be thrown down." He had also intimated the cessation of the temple worship, in that saying to the woman of Samaria. "Woman, believe Me, the hour cometh, when ye shall neither in this mountain, nor yet at Jerusalem, worship the Father."

In truth, the principle established by Stephen follows of necessity from the incarnation of the Son of God. If God should ever set up a tabernacle in human flesh, and make a temple of man's body, it is clear that no spot on earth and no house made with hands could thenceforth be so sacred as the body in which He had dwelt. The living man in whom God dwells and lives and speaks, must be a holier and more real temple than any fabric of dead stone and timber, however costly and beautiful it may be. If a living thing is holy, it must be holier than the dead.

Here is another reason why it is important to remember Stephen. It is not only that he is the first martyr; he is a martyr to the principle which was established by our Lord's incarnation, that "the most High dwelleth not in temples made with hands." The reason why He commanded that temples should be made with hands for Him before, was that He might draw men's thoughts to the fact that He did intend to dwell and walk among men.

The tent and tabernacle in which He walked in the wilderness, as well as the temple of Solomon, were really figures of Christ's humanity. We can never study them to much purpose unless we regard them in that way. When the real temple came, "the temple of His body," it was time for the shadows to pass away. Whether Stephen had openly said this, or not, his Master had certainly foretold it, and it was true.

HOLY PLACES

And this being so, we cannot be surprised to find that Stephen never directly contradicted the charge which the false witnesses made against him. He did not, like our Lord before Caiaphas, keep silence, and leave his adversaries to prove what they could. Nor did he exactly deny it. He met it, full of the Holy Ghost, and stood in the midst of the great council, with his face shining like an angel's, and with the eye of his mind, no doubt, seeing much further into the matter of dispute than the mere technical meaning of the charge.

And so when the accusers ceased, and the High Priest having heard what they had to say, and being somewhat awed by the countenance of the prisoner before him, put the hesitating question, "Are these things then really so?" Stephen, being put on his defense, entered into the matter fully, and set before the Jewish council the whole teaching of the Old Testament with regard to sacred places, besides a great deal that tended to establish the fact that Jesus was the Christ.

To read Stephen's speech now, as Stephen himself delivered it, is a task quite beyond our powers. Some things may perhaps be brought out by emphasis, after careful thought and study. But to prove the truth of what is said, you have only to go over it as it stands, reading it as an ordinary reader would deliver it, and ask yourself, "What in the world did it contain that could provoke the audience to stone the speaker on the spot?" They took no more time to perceive the meaning than was spent in hearing the words. They stopped their ears before it was ended, "and ran upon him with one accord."

Without a very considerable effort of thought and imagination it is not possible to see why.

Now, without pretending to explain this difficulty, I will ask you to go through this speech with me, noting all the allusions to places which it contains. Thus we may partly see how Stephen met the charge of want of reverence for sacred places, of which his enemies complained. Every turn of the speech is full of beauty. But let us direct our attention to that one line of thought.

And he said, "Brethren and fathers, hearken. The God of glory" (who is surely free to display His glory where He will) "appeared unto our father Abraham, when he was in Mesopotamia, before he dwelt in Charran." He did not wait for him to leave the land of the Chaldeans, much less to leave Haran, and enter the Holy Land. The God of glory appeared in Mesopotamia. There He first called our father Abraham, and bade him, "Get thee out of thy country, and from thy kindred, and from thy father's house, unto a land (whatsoever land) that I shall show thee." But He did not at once lead Abraham to Canaan. He directed his steps to Haran, the city of Nahor, as it was afterwards called.

And not until Terah's death did God remove Abraham into this land (said Stephen) wherein ye now dwell. "And He gave him none inheritance in it, no, not so much as to set his foot on: yet He promised that He would give it to him for a possession."

Where was the Holy place *then,* when Abraham sojourned in the land of promise as in a strange country, "dwelling in tabernacles with Isaac and Jacob, the heirs with him of the same promise?" Did not the very lack of a fixed abode and place of worship direct the patriarch's expectation to "the city which hath foundations, whose builder and maker is God?"

But further, "God spake on this wise," that Abraham's seed should be sojourners, "strangers and pilgrims like their father in a strange land." And they should also be brought into bondage and afflicted and all this until the completion of a period of "four hundred years," *i.e,* from the time those words were said.

"And the nation to whom they shall be in bondage will I judge, said God: and after that shall they come forth, and serve Me in this place." In this place. What place? If those very words were so spoken to Abraham, it would be in Canaan. If, however, this is what our reference Bibles make it, an allusion to later words addressed to Moses on Sinai, "Ye shall serve God upon this mountain," it is another place of worship.

I believe that the confusion between Sinai and Canaan here is intentional. It points to that which Paul has brought out plainly in his Epistle to the Galatians, where he says that Mount Sinai in Arabia "answereth to Jerusalem which now is, and is in bondage with her children." And if Stephen contrived to suggest that comparison to his audience, it could not have been exactly an acceptable suggestion.

But to proceed. Through the lives of Abraham, Isaac, and Jacob, we are led rapidly on to the time when "the patriarchs, moved with envy, sold Joseph into Egypt: but God was with him." Thither, in the course of providence, all his people followed him, and took up their abode in the very center of the great Gentile power of the day. Was not Egypt a sacred place in the time of Joseph?

It was the cradle of the Hebrew nation, when Israel was "God's son, even His firstborn." It was also the refuge of the infant Saviour, of whom Israel, in that relation to Jehovah, was a type. In Egypt then, Jacob and Joseph and the rest of the patriarchs died. But where were they buried? Stephen here, by no mistake as is rashly maintained, but well knowing what he was talking about, omits all mention of the place of Jacob's burial, Hebron in the land of Judea. He brings out the fact, which was far less pleasing to his hearers and much more to the purpose for his argument, that Joseph and his brethren were buried in Sychem. That is, in Samaria, in a sepulcher which Abraham had bought, more than fifty years before he bought the cave of Machpelah, in which he and Isaac and Jacob were laid.

The fifteenth and sixteenth verses should be read thus: "And Jacob went down into Egypt and died, he and our fathers; and they (not Jacob, but Joseph and his brethren, the fathers of the other tribes) "were carried over into Sychem (not Hebron), and buried in the sepulcher that Abraham (not Jacob) had bought for a sum of money of the sons of Emmor the son (not the father) of Sychem." Those who charge Stephen with a mistake here, not only show their disrespect for the speaker, but spoil the whole point of his argument.

Imagine the disgust of the Jewish council of this period, at being reminded that the bones of all the patriarchs

HOLY PLACES

after Jacob, were interred in Samaria!

However, the speaker immediately returns to Egypt, and continues the narrative. He reminds us almost immediately that Moses, the great prophet, ruler, and deliverer of Israel, was born there. Moreover, he was brought up in Pharaoh's court as a learned Egyptian, the son of Pharaoh's daughter. From thence, on the failure of his first attempt to deliver Israel, he fled to the land of Midian. There, in due time, he was favored with a most marvelous revelation of Jehovah's presence, which has ever since been a standing type of all His earthly dwelling places. The Angel of Jehovah appeared to Moses in the wilderness of Sinai in a flame of fire in a bush.

The same good will which was manifested in Mesopotamia and Charran, and Egypt and Samaria, is now made manifest in the wilderness of Sinai, in a flame of fire in a bush; the figure of God's people in suffering, which makes every place where that figure is realized to be holy ground. The treatment of Moses by Israel is described and commented upon severely. But on that part of the speech of Stephen I do not now dwell.

He brings Israel and Moses to God at Sinai, as he had brought them through Joseph into Egypt. And in both places alike it might have been said, "I bare you on eagles' wings, and brought you unto Myself." He also alludes to the manifestations of the Divine power and presence "in Egypt and in the Red Sea, and in the wilderness forty years."

One more note of place occurs in the speech, and it is

a very remarkable one. It is not the place of worship but the place of captivity. "I will carry you away *beyond Babylon*" (v. 43). The Old Testament prophet Amos, from whom the words are cited, said, *"beyond Damascus."* Stephen, also a prophet, varies the message to suit the need of the time. "Beyond Babylon," he says, Israel shall go. And yet in Babylon, the God of glory was revealed. Elisha was sent to Damascus. But Jehovah Himself walked with the three Jewish martyrs in the midst of the burning fiery furnace, "in the plain of Dura in the province of Babylon." In the same place, I suppose, He also sat with Daniel in the lions' den. Even when Israel should be carried "beyond Babylon," is it not written, "If from thence thou shalt seek the Lord thy God, thou shalt find Him, if thou seek Him with all thy heart and with all thy soul."

Turn back once more to the charge made against Stephen, and see how he has met it. "We have heard him say that Jesus of Nazareth shall destroy this place." What place? Do you mean the city of Jerusalem, the place which the Lord hath chosen, or do you mean the temple, the place of worship? Take which you will. Say Jerusalem first. You charge me with saying He will destroy it. And what if He did? Is Jerusalem the only place in which men can meet with God and be saved? What of Mesopotamia and Haran and Egypt and Samaria, and Sinai, and the Red Sea, and the wilderness? Yes, and Babylon, too? Were not each and all of these at one time or another holy ground?

Or do you mean the temple, the place of worship? As

HOLY PLACES

regards this he would say, there was a time when the temple itself was not. "Our fathers had the tabernacle of witness in the wilderness" (v. 44). That was made at Sinai, and borne from place to place for forty years; made in order to travel. Joshua and his successors in Canaan for several centuries had nothing more. Even David, favored as he was in many respects, "desired to find a tabernacle for the God of Jacob," but desired in vain. For it was "Solomon built Him an house."

Now what follows from all this? What can possibly follow, but what Stephen adds—using the words of Isaiah to confirm the statement. "Howbeit the Most High dwelleth not in temples made with hands; as saith the prophet." "Heaven is My throne" a seat of praise but not My only one; "and the earth it is a footstool. What house will ye build Me...or what is the place of My rest? Hath not My hand made all these things?" He might have added what Isaiah adds in that place, an intimation that man is God's true temple. "For all those things hath Mine hand made...but to this man will I look, even to him that is poor and of a contrite spirit, and trembleth at My word" (Isa. 66:2).

In another similar passage in Isaiah 57:15, we are brought to the same conclusion. "Thus saith the high and lofty One that inhabiteth eternity, whose name is Holy; I dwell in the high and holy place, with him also that is of a contrite and humble spirit, to revive the spirit of the humble, and to revive the heart of the contrite ones."

Thus did Stephen meet the charge made against him, the charge of irreverence towards God's holy place. He met it by pointing out that no place on earth has (so to speak) a monopoly of God's presence and blessing; that His last and greatest temple is man. This is the great fact established by the incarnation, that God desires to dwell in man, and invites man to dwell in Him.

Before leaving the subject, I should like to say a word upon the other part of the charge mentioned in the text. "We have heard him say, that Jesus of Nazareth shall…change the customs which Moses delivered us." By those customs they meant of course the religious rites, as the margin of our Bibles reminds us. But the word for customs is perfectly general and may mean any customs whatever.

Now there was one custom thought to have been delivered by Moses, which was so entirely changed by Jesus of Nazareth and His first martyr Stephen that we cannot but notice it here. "Ye have heard that it hath been said by them of old time, Thou shalt love thy neighbor and hate thine enemy." I cannot find among the customs delivered by Moses any rule that a man should pray for his murderers, as did our Lord when He said, "Father, forgive them," or as Stephen did with his last cry.

There is something particularly beautiful in the way this comes out in the story of the death of Stephen. In chapter 7:59, we read, "they stoned Stephen, calling upon God, and saying…." The word *God* in that place is not in the original. It is literally, "they stoned Stephen appealing, and saying…" With the very same word Stephen's successor removed his cause out of the hands of all the judges in the land of Israel, saying, "I appeal unto

Caesar." But they stoned Stephen without a sentence, and in the act of appeal; appealing not to Caesar but to the King of kings; "appealing and saying, Lord Jesus receive my spirit."

The martyrs have always had that right of appeal. From the blood of Abel, which cried to Jehovah from the ground, to the blood of Zacharias who was stoned between the altar and the temple, saying, "The Lord look upon it and require it" (2 Chron. 24:22). Yes, and even to the last of those who are "slain for the Word of God, and for the testimony that they held," whose souls cry from under the altar, "How long, O Lord, holy and true, dost Thou not judge and avenge our blood on them that dwell on the earth"—the martyrs have always had that right of appeal. So did Stephen appeal and say, "Lord Jesus, I am oppressed, undertake for me, and receive my spirit."

But no sooner had the appeal passed his lips, than there came back upon his parting breath the spirit of his Master; and the appeal for vengeance became an appeal for mercy. Louder than he had spoken for himself, he cried out for those who slew him, "Lord, lay not this sin to their charge." And then "he fell asleep."

And thus was one more earthly temple of Jehovah taken down and removed to a better world. With his dying breath, Stephen proved that a mortal man may himself be the temple of the living God, the Holy One of Israel. Never more surely and remarkably so, than when the indwelling spirit of Jesus turns the appeal for justice to ourselves, into a cry for pardon for those who deal unjustly, whom none but our Saviour Himself could have taught us to forgive like this.

In this way we all have abundant opportunities of proving that man may be God's temple, by manifesting the spirit of Jesus in all those trials which seem to afford special provocation to the words and works of the flesh. May God give His Holy Spirit thus to dwell in us, and make us His habitation for evermore.

CHAPTER FIVE

BEARING THE CURSE

Verily, verily, I say unto you, If a man keep My saying, he shall never see death.
JOHN 8:51

It would seem that our Lord said this of Himself, as the strongest possible form of denial that He could give to the insulting accusation of His enemies. "Say we not well that thou art a Samaritan, and hast a devil?" The devil, he had just reminded them, was a liar and a murderer from the beginning, aiming at the lives of men. Our Lord was manifested that He might destroy the works of the devil, meeting the devil's lie by His own testimony to the truth, and defeating the devil's murderous devices, by destroying his power as lord of death. We have heard of the fall of man, and then of the death of the Saviour for our salvation: the assault on man's life by Satan, and the triumph won by our Lord upon the cross. By that victory, "He became the author of eternal salvation unto all them that obey Him." He justified His own declaration, that, "If a man keep My saying, he shall never see death."

SHADOWS OF REDEMPTION

I want to invite your attention to the way in which this truth is presented in the third chapter of Genesis, the way of salvation as it is foretold and foreshadowed there. I want to be more thoroughly convinced myself, and to more thoroughly convince you, that there is the most perfect and entire safety for us when we put ourselves into the hands of Christ, that it is no mere figure of speech, but the very truth of God, that if we follow His direction, we shall never see death.

I do not propose to dwell on the falsehood, by which Satan contrived to strike his deadly blow. In the plainest language possible, God had said of the tree of knowledge to Adam, "In the day that thou eatest thereof thou shalt surely die," *i.e.,* "By dying thou wilt die," that will be the natural effect of eating. It will put you off the path of life, and set your feet in the way of death, not necessarily sudden and instantaneous death, but you will die by dying, you will lose more of life daily, and will in the end lose all. Perhaps, also, the words may mean, "By the death of thy body you will also come to the death of the spirit, a second death. You will be cut off from communion with the Lord of Life. And by thus dying, you will indeed die." This was the threat. None of us know, thank God, its full meaning. May we need never know it!

But, be it what it may, the tempter contradicted it, saying, "Ye shall not surely die." You will not die by dying. You will either not die at all, or if you do die, you will not die of it. You will be none the worse. Rather you will find yourselves wiser and better off than you now are.

The lie prevailed upon the woman. The woman pre-

BEARING THE CURSE

vailed over the man. And the adversary had his way.

But the Creator was not taken by surprise. As a good shepherd who knew that his sheep might go astray, He came to visit them. "And they heard the voice of the Lord God walking in the garden in the cool of the day." Let me read it as the Jews of our Lord's time were taught to read it. "They heard the voice of the Word of the Lord God, Jehovah Elohim, walking in the garden in the quiet of the day. And Adam and his wife hid themselves from Jehovah Elohim, in the midst of the trees of the garden." Here for the first time we find the second Person of the Trinity called by that striking name with which the Apostle John has made us familiar, "the Word of the Lord."

It might have been a recollection of this very verse that crossed his mind when he wrote, "In the beginning was the Word," and "the Word was God." They heard the voice of the Word of Jehovah walking. They hid themselves, he continues, from Jehovah Himself. The Word was Jehovah, and it was the Word who was made flesh. The same Word, who came to seek fallen men in the midst of Eden, came again in the likeness of man to seek him, when he was like a lost sheep in the wilderness, in the world where Paradise had almost faded out of memory, a world that was anything but the garden of the Lord.

Speedily was the tale of man's calamity unbosomed in the presence of the Word of the Lord. From Adam He traced it to the woman, and from the woman to the serpent. And then He at once declared His judgment, beginning with the most guilty. The Lord God said unto the serpent (Gen. 3:14-15), "Because thou hast done this, thou art cursed above all cattle, and above every beast of the field; upon thy belly shalt thou go, and dust shalt thou eat all the days of thy life; and I will put enmity between thee and the woman, and between thy seed and her seed; it shall bruise thy head and thou shalt bruise his heel."

To the woman He said, "I will greatly multiply thy sorrow and thy conception; in sorrow thou shalt bring forth children; and thy desire shall be to thy husband, and he shall rule over thee."

And to Adam He said, "Because thou hast hearkened unto the voice of thy wife, and hast eaten of the tree of which I commanded thee…saying, Thou shalt not eat of it: cursed is the ground for thy sake; in sorrow shalt thou eat of it all the days of thy life; thorns also and thistles shall it bring forth to thee; and thou shalt eat the herb of the field; in the sweat of thy face shalt thou eat bread, till thou return unto the ground; for out of it wast thou taken: for dust thou art, and unto dust shalt thou return."

Does all this sound like an utterance that had not been premeditated? However easy to the Divine wisdom to pronounce all this, when we realize what it entailed on Him who said it, we cannot but acknowledge that He had planned it all before. In fact, it was all contained in the possibilities of that design which He expressed before He made us, "Let Us make man…after Our likeness." That could not be without temptation. And the fact of temptation means the possibility of a fall.

Let us notice here, that the very thing to be dreaded as a consequence of the fall—the thing threatened when God forbade the fruit of the tree of knowledge, the fear-

BEARING THE CURSE

ful thing called *death*—is the one thing not named in the sentence of the Word of the Lord. Why? Because that word was not the sentence of death, but rather the promise of life. Because of that—no less than of all His other sayings—it is true, that "if a man keep My saying, he shall never see death."

In the threefold doom which the word of the Lord pronounced on the three offenders in Paradise, He was really passing sentence upon Himself. He sketched there in outline that which He had undertaken to do.

First in relation to the serpent, that curse which He spoke with His mouth, He also fulfilled with His hand. The enmity which He foretold between the serpent and the woman was a quarrel that He maintained Himself. He then and there undertook to meet every lying profession of friendship on the part of the devil, with a faithful exposure by the light of His own truth, that no delusion of Satan might ever be able permanently to hold its ground.

As for the seed of the woman, He became that seed Himself. He set His own heel upon the serpent, bruising it sorely, while He crushed the serpent's head. As Moses lifted up the serpent in the wilderness, so even then the Son of Man undertook to "be lifted up, that whosoever believeth in Him should not perish, but have eternal life" (Jn. 3:14-16).

Take the next part of the sentence, that which He pronounced upon the woman. And let no man be surprised to learn that our Lord suffered for men and women. When God created man in His own image, it is written, that, "male and female created He them." To both man and woman alike belongs the name of Adam (Gen. 5:1-2). "He blessed them, and called *their* name Adam." As the first Adam contained in himself the whole sum of humanity, so does the last Adam. In Jesus Christ there is neither Jew nor Gentile, neither male nor female. There is neither, because here are both. And as both Jew and Gentile in Him find perfect sympathy, so that He cannot possibly be more to the one than He is to the other, being all-sufficient for both, so is He in His relation to man and woman.

He has borne the griefs and carried the sorrows of the weaker vessel, no less than of the stronger, and that especially in His mediatorial relation between man and God. Paul draws the parallels thus, "The head of every man is Christ; and the head of every woman is the man; and the head of Christ is God."

Had this truth always been realized, that the love of Christ passes the love of woman as well as the love of man, there had been no temptation to worship His mother. He Himself is quite enough. It was necessary that in Him as in the first Adam, all elements of man's nature should have their part. And therefore we shall find that He has taken upon Himself the burden laid upon the woman in man's fall.

Christ laid no burden on any woman on earth except His mother. But in the redemption of all His children, in bearing them to their heavenly Father, He has borne the mother's burden Himself. Of all the great multitude of the redeemed together, it is written, "These are they which came out of the great tribulation," a tribulation that is not

BEARING THE CURSE

theirs but His. And if their robes are washed and made white in the light of His presence, they are "made white in the blood of the Lamb."

That very word *tribulation,* as used in the New Testament, has a special association with the pangs of labor and of birth. Our Lord Himself used it on the night of His betrayal. Yet, like Himself, He applied it to the lesser sufferings of His disciples, as though forgetful of His own. "A woman when she is in travail (He said) hath sorrow, because her hour is come: but as soon as she is delivered of the child, she remembereth no more the anguish (the tribulation), for joy that a man is born into the world. And ye now therefore have sorrow." Might He not more truly have said, "I now therefore have sorrow"? What was their sorrow to His sorrow?

> *O, all ye that pass by, behold and see!*
> *Man stole the fruit; but I must climb the tree,*
> *The tree of life to all, save only Me;*
> *Was ever grief like Mine?*

The same figure of tribulation is used, though not in the same fulness of meaning, by Paul, who suffered almost more than man could bear in the birth of the Church. "My little children, of whom I travail in birth again until Christ be formed in you," he said to the Galatians. And again in his epistle to the Colossians, "Who now rejoice in my sufferings for you, and fill up that which is behind of the afflictions of Christ" (as it were the after-pains that remained of His great tribulation) "in my flesh for His body's sake, which is the

Church." At the cost of those pains, the Church was born, not of the bondwoman like Ishmael, but, like Isaac, of Jerusalem that is free.

One other great tribulation is described in the same way, that which shall precede the second birth of Israel in the latter days. Their great tribulation is the time of the birth-pangs of their nation. But the sum of all these sufferings is found in the tribulation of Jesus Christ. At His resurrection were "loosed the birth-pangs of His death," to use the remarkable language of Peter on the day of Pentecost. And in His great agony we see how His desire was subject to the Father of His many sons who were to be born to glory, when He said in meek submission to that trying hour, "Father, if Thou be willing, remove this cup from Me: nevertheless not My will but Thine be done."

There is still the third sentence to be noticed, which was pronounced on Adam. Here truly the Son of Man had the inheritance of His adopted father. Over the cursed ground He walked in weariness, and found it no more fruitful to Him than it was to others. Where He sowed good seed, the enemy came and sowed tares, and both grew together in a tangle inextricable until the harvest. And even of the good seed; some fell by the wayside, and some fell on the rock, and some among the thorns. Very little brought forth fruit that would "remain."

Thorns of the wilderness were woven for the crown they gave Him when He had run His race. Who else ever ate so continually the bread of sorrows? As the herb of the field, appointed for the beasts before, was assigned to

BEARING THE CURSE

man when fallen, "Thou shalt eat the herb of the field," so we read that our Lord when He came to seek fruit found "nothing but leaves." Or the blade sprang up after His sowing, and died before it brought forth fruit, and that not only in the natural world, but in reality again and again. In the sweat of His face did He eat bread while He lived. He was often hungry and thirsty and weary in the wilderness. And before He died, "His sweat was as it were great drops of blood falling down to the ground."

At last they brought Him to the dust of death. And then, having exhausted His own sentence, and fulfilled His own sayings, He arose, "a second man, the Lord from heaven," the Adam of the redeemed race. Having been obedient until death, and learned the whole obedience by the things He suffered, He became the Author of eternal salvation to all them that obey Him. And thus He justified, to the very uttermost, His wonderful reply to the insults of the Jews, "Verily, verily, I say unto you, If a man keep My saying, He shall never see death."

Now is not that saying true? "He shall never see death." Is not Christ, in His life and death for us, a shield for us from the dreadful sentence that we incurred by that act of disobedience at the first? "Whosoever liveth and believeth in Me shall never die." What is Christ's saying that we should keep? He bids us come to Him and intrust ourselves to Him, putting our lives into His hand. He invites us to become "members of His body, of His flesh, and of His bones." Not of that body which had still to suffer and die, but of that which "is raised from the dead" and dies no more. "Death hath no more dominion over it."

We may be called upon to submit to the bruising of the serpent in us. We may, no, we must be called to tribulation. The pangs of the new birth are necessary for all who enter into the kingdom of God. But, at the most, it is only "that which is behind of the afflictions of Christ." We have the assurance and comfort of His presence and experience, in every pang we are called to undergo. We never have to suffer alone as He had. The toil of man's daily life is consecrated. The very thorns of the wilderness are now the symbol of His victory. May they never crowd out His word from our hearts, in the shape of worldly anxieties and cares! All anxiety is forbidden, where there is room for prayer to Him.

And the return of these bodies to the dust is not death. Our Saviour has given us many better names for it than that. Man's strength may "fail," and he may have to "tarry" in weakness for the summons of his Master, and then lie down to "sleep" for a time, before he rises up to immortal youth and vigor, but "whosoever liveth and believeth in Christ shall never die."

Even that part of death in which Old Testament saints could never see any brightness, the intermediate state between death and resurrection—is lighted up for us by the prospect of departing to be with Christ in Paradise, a thing far, far higher than the fullest tide of life here, though it be but half the incorruptible inheritance of the life to come. Look at it which way you will, is it not a true word of our Saviour's, "If a man keep My saying, he shall never see death"? Contrast it with the lying promise of the tempter, "Ye shall not surely die." Not surely die—no,

BEARING THE CURSE

but never feel sure of life. For what is your life here? "It is even a vapor." And without Christ what is there to look to beyond?

But the promise of Christ, how different! To be held in the hollow of His hand here. "If I live, I live for the Lord, and if I die, I die for the Lord," and live with Him forever. As it is written in the Proverbs, "In the way of righteousness is life; and in the pathway thereof is no death." Begin to walk upon it, and you will see signs of life around you, before you, and on either side. By and by, on that road you will see footsteps. A track is before you and an example. You follow this, and it narrows into a pathway, and a bright light shines at the end. That is the light of immortality, the pathway to the house of no-death. Not merely the escape from darkness and peril, but the certain prospect of "the inheritance incorruptible, and an undefiled…crown of glory that fadeth not away," the fulness of life and vigor in a better world.

And what is the beginning of that way? It is just keeping the word of Jesus Christ. It is to put yourself into His hand, and trust Him, to hear His voice, and to cling to Him daily for direction, not only to hope for His salvation at the last.

"If a man keep My saying." What is He saying to each of us? "Come unto Me," is His first saying. "Take My yoke upon you, and learn of Me," is the next. To learn of Him you must go to Him daily: you cannot learn much by only going once a week. If you want to learn, you must learn every day, and practice what you learn. Oh, let us learn more and more of what Christ will teach us.

SHADOWS OF REDEMPTION

He walked in the garden of Eden, and called our first parents, as if He did not know, or would not think, that they had sinned. He walks still in the midst of all the churches, although He knows our works. He even says, "I will dwell in them, and walk in them." Ask Him to dwell and walk in you. He was appointed our Lord and Master for this very purpose, that He might guide us, and that we might learn of Him.

How can we "do all in the Name of the Lord Jesus," if we cannot call on Him and hear Him every hour? "Let the word of Christ dwell in you richly in all wisdom." Cling to Him until you can hear Him daily, and learn to keep His commandments and abide in His love.

And then it shall be true of you far more than of our first parents; "My sheep hear My voice, and I know them, and they follow Me. And I give unto them eternal life; and they shall never perish, neither shall any man pluck them out of My hand."

CHAPTER SIX

IN ALL POINTS TEMPTED

For we have not an high priest which cannot be touched with the feeling of our infirmities; but was in all points tempted like as we are, yet without sin.
Hebrews 4:15

Here are three things in which we can see that our Lord Jesus Christ has been brought near to fallen men, *viz.,* in the possession of our common humanity, in temptation, and in prayer. Of all three we find the most numerous proofs and examples in the Gospel according to Luke, the Gospel which sets Him forth to us more especially as the Son of Man.

There we find the tokens of His humanity in all the details of His nativity; in the one solitary incident recorded of the days of His boyhood and in the repeated mention of His growth in wisdom and stature; in the many sayings of His ministerial life that betoken sympathy with ordinary human nature. In the stories of the unjust judge, the unjust steward, the friend moved by importunity rather than by friendship, the prodigal son, and other well-known passages of Luke's Gospel, we see that He who received sinners and ate with them, knew also what sinners were.

In that Gospel more than in any other, we find proofs of His sense of the deep need of human nature, in that He was so constantly in prayer. These instances we may easily collect. And if the incidents told us by Luke only, in the narrative of our Lord's sufferings and death, are brought together, we may easily see there how He was made even "lower than the angels" that He might sympathize with the infirmities of man. But the place where He came nearest to man was in temptation. He "was in all points tempted like as we are." One thing seems most essential in order to grasp the teaching and the comfort of this verse, and that is to feel sure that it is true. If we expressed what many of us feel in our secret hearts, we should say, "I believe the fact because the Bible says so. But I do not see that Christ was in all points tempted like as I am, and I should find great comfort in this saying, if I could see how it is true."

To obtain a complete view of our Lord's temptations, let us divide them into four parts.

There was first of all what we may call His private life as a simple Israelite, His life at Nazareth as the son of Joseph and Mary, the carpenter's son, and then the carpenter (when Joseph died)—His life until He was about thirty years old.

Concerning the temptations of this part of His life,

IN ALL POINTS TEMPTED

the Gospel is silent. But we know that there were temptations, because we know that He was man. Even in Paradise, man was not to live without temptation. If not in Paradise, much less at Nazareth, a place which had not a good character among the inhabitants of Galilee, who were "sitters in darkness," compared with those who dwelt in other parts of the Holy Land. "Can there any good thing come out of Nazareth?" said one whose personal character made him a competent judge.

We know of one temptation presented to our Lord at that period. It was the temptation to forsake Nazareth for Jerusalem, to be continually in the temple occupied upon the study of Scripture, and in holy things; to be about the business of His Father in heaven, rather than about the plows and yokes and other implements of husbandry, which we are told He learned to make, from the man whom He called father upon earth.

The second part of His experience of temptation was when He had been baptized. He was then acknowledged by "the voice of one crying in the wilderness," and the voice that spake from heaven, as the Son of God, the Lamb that "taketh away the sin of the world." The Holy Spirit, in a bodily form, descended on Him, and immediately drove Him forth into the wilderness, there to meet the Evil One in person. He was tempted forty days and forty nights, and then most sharply tempted when they were over, in a way that searched His principles to their very foundation.

Those three temptations in the wilderness, on which we will not now dwell, were enough to try the intelligence of the wisest servant of God. We know from an expression in Luke 4, that there was here a complete course of temptation. It is literally, "When the devil had ended all the temptations," when He had wound up or consummated all temptation, every temptation. Then, and not till then, did the tempter stand aside and withdraw. Because he had tried all that he knew, he withdrew from our Saviour "for a season," literally "until a certain time," until a convenient season, until another opportunity should present itself when he might try again with additional force.

The season when the tempter returned is noted by our Saviour in John 14:30. "Hereafter I will not talk much with you: for the prince of this world cometh, and hath nothing in Me." But we are not to suppose that the intervening time, the time of our Lord's ministry, was free from temptation: He Himself is witness that it was far otherwise. What did He say to His disciples on the night of the last supper"? Ye are they which have continued with Me in My temptations" (Lk. 22:28). What temptations?

Not the temptations of His private life at Nazareth, for then He had no disciples. Most of the twelve had not known Him till He called them to follow His steps. Not the temptation in the wilderness. That was immediately after His baptism. There was no witness there. "Angels ministered unto Him," when that hour was over. No disciples watched with Him while the conflict was going on. Then what does He mean by saying to the disciples, "Ye have continued with Me in My temptations"? It can only

IN ALL POINTS TEMPTED

be of His ministry that He speaks. When they came to Him, He had already passed two stages of temptation.

When He spoke these words, the last and worst hour of temptation was yet to come. These words must therefore refer to the days of His ministry. We call it His ministry. He called it "My temptations." This was the only name that He gave to that period of His life.

But what a summary it is of those days and weeks spent in going about doing good, casting out devils, healing sick folk, preaching, teaching, conversing, receiving. The things He did and said in those days, "many prophets and kings" had "desired to see...and had not seen" or heard them. The brief record of them in the Gospel has held the attention of mankind from that day till now.

Yet what was it to Him who went through it? What recollection did it leave on His mind? *My temptations.* What a commentary on the Gospel is wrapped up in those words, if we could unfold and read it. For every step He took, was He not tempted to take another which might have been easier and looked likely to be more successful?

For every healing work He wrought, was He not tempted to another, more likely to win Him favor with the world? For every true word He spoke, was He not tempted to speak another, more likely to please His hearers, more calculated to exalt the speaker in the eyes of Israel, only not quite so true? For every work that He performed with labor, was it not suggested to Him that He might have found an easier way? When He rejoined His disciples on the Sea of Galilee in that most wonderful act of His life, why need He have walked thither over the uneven waves, unsheltered in the face of the same wind that was contrary to them?

Even in that most awe-inspiring and God-like of miracles, He had a large share of human toil. To understand the temptations of our Lord's ministry, we must try to put ourselves into His place, and imagine ourselves to be possessed of His power. But what child of man ever had the thousandth part of the power and wielded it as He did? The self-restraint of our Lord's ministry was itself a constant miracle.

It was Almighty power wielded by human nature, in obedience to Divine will. In truth we cannot understand these temptations of His ministry, until we have fathomed the mind and purpose of God respecting men. To make man "after the Divine likeness" was the task. When we know what that likeness is, we shall see the glory of the skill that made it. But there is matter for study to all eternity, in the principles and methods of our Lord's life.

In the other world, they who see Him and His redeemed may hear the "many other things" He did, which have not been written; things that would tax the world's capacity to receive or understand. And, remember, every thing that our Lord did and said in the course of His ministry, implied temptation, the temptation to do it for the glory of man. This He might have done in a hundred different ways instead of choosing the one way which He selected, or rather which He received from His Father, the way by which man must learn to follow the glory of God.

Three chapters of temptation we have now noticed:

IN ALL POINTS TEMPTED

1) The temptations of the private life of Jesus of Nazareth; 2) The first great assault of Satan in the wilderness (itself a complete course of temptation); 3) the innumerable temptations of His ministerial life.

The fourth chapter is still before us, "the hour and power of darkness." That there was to be a last great Satanic effort is clear beforehand from the Gospel. Once the devil had withdrawn, until he should find his opportunity.

Our Lord felt his approach on the night of His betrayal. He warned the disciples of it. "Simon, Simon, behold Satan hath desired to have you, that be may sift you as wheat." He warned them again in Gethsemane to "rise and pray" lest they entered "into temptation," while He agonized in prayer Himself.

The intensity of His preparation for the conflict showed what the conflict was to be. And what was it? Wherein did this last assault differ from all previous assaults upon our Lord? Not in the things propounded by the tempter, we may be sure. He had already propounded every deviation that was conceivable from the narrow way of holiness, the redemption of man into obedience to the will of God.

But the last temptation differed from all the former in this respect. It was temptation under the torture. When cruel men have had their fellow-men within their power, and have sought to bend them to their will, they have been known first to try bribes, and wiles and promises, and when all these failed, to resort to other means.

The body has been stretched upon the rack in extremity of pain, while the things that the oppressors desired were propounded to the victim. As evil men have dealt with their fellow-men, so by the hands of wicked men did Satan at last deal with our Lord.

In order to realize this, you must remember who urged His crucifixion and on what grounds. It was His own people who clamored for His life. But remember why they did so. It was because, while claiming to be their Messiah and Saviour, He would not reign and save them in the way they wanted. They had no personal animosity to Him, if He would have done the things they liked. Remember, that, at any stage of the proceedings, a few words from the lips of Jesus of Nazareth would have changed the blaspheming enemies into willing slaves. Had He but said, "Stay; I have led you thus far to try you; I see you are faithful to your religion, which God gave you by Moses. Now I will give you as the reward of your faithfulness whatever you desire. Behold the sign from heaven you have often requested. Now gird ye on every man his sword and follow Me to victory. In a few moments your oppressors shall be crushed beneath us, and all Palestine, nay, all the empire of the world, shall be your own."

A few words such as these, accompanied by a single miracle, would have made peace between Jesus and the Jewish authorities. And even at a later stage of the proceedings, Pontius Pilate would have been only too glad to escape the responsibility which Jewish fanaticism thrust upon him, of condemning the innocent. Even if our Lord disdained to accept the homage of the Jews for their

IN ALL POINTS TEMPTED

meanness and narrowness and unworthiness, might He not have turned to the Romans? A few words spoken to Pilate when He asked "Whence art thou?" a promise of Divine protection enforced with one touch of Almighty power, would have saved Jesus from the cross. Or if Jew and Roman were alike unworthy, remember the other resource that our Saviour mentioned in His own words, "Thinkest thou that I cannot now pray to My Father, and He shall presently give Me more than twelve legions of angels? But how then shall the Scriptures be fulfilled, that thus it must be?" What other reason was there for enduring the torture of the Cross?

And now let us return to our text. "We have not an High Priest which cannot be touched with the feeling of our infirmities, but was in all points tempted like as we are, yet without sin." "Tempted like as we are," does it say? O, but which of us has ever been tempted like Him?

Have we exhausted all the possibilities of even one of our Lord's four chapters of temptations? The thirty years at Nazareth, the forty days in the wilderness, the three years of ceaseless activity in public, the one night and day of protracted torture, torture which at any moment might have ceased forever if He had but spoken the word! What have we ever had to endure that can compare with that? Bodily pain and weariness, the struggles of poverty, suggestions of compromise with the world, worldly ways of doing good, harmless ways of self-indulgence; which is there of all these that oppresses us, which has not been far more strongly pressed upon Him?

Indeed, which of us has ever been the object of a distinct personal assault by the Prince of Darkness? To say nothing of a complete course of temptation, which of us is so strong, so holy, as to make it worthwhile for the Evil One to bestow his personal attention on us at all? An old sinful habit is enough for one, a provoking word will trip up another, the pressure of a little bodily inconvenience will excuse a third, a little prospect of gain overpowers a fourth, and so on. "We have not yet resisted unto blood, striving against sin." He did.

And have we ever really thought in our secret souls that our trials and temptations can press us more than His? God forgive our foolishness and our blindness, that we cannot see a little further into this matter. Let us ask Him to "anoint our eyes with eye-salve that we may see." And then let us address ourselves once more to the two practical duties with which our text is linked by the words before and after. One is to "hold fast our (Christian) profession," and another is to "come boldly unto the throne of grace." To "hold fast" lest we disgrace that most noble example. To "come boldly unto the throne" where He sits, whose experience of victory is no less infinite than His experience of suffering through temptation to sin—and whose compassion and sympathy matches, in its infinitude, the other two.

CHAPTER SEVEN

IN THE WILDERNESS

*Then was Jesus led up of the Spirit into the wilderness
to be tempted of the devil.*
MATTHEW 4:1

We read in the New Testament that our Lord Jesus Christ was "in all points tempted like as we are," and therefore we do not doubt that He experienced the ordinary temptations which are "common to man" during those thirty years of His life of which the New Testament gives us no history.

But this is the first time that we read in the Gospel of His being tempted. This temptation in the wilderness was not ordinary temptation. It could not be said of this that it was "common to man." And this being extraordinary temptation, we may suppose that our Lord was specially prepared for it. His human nature needed some preparation. He may be compared to the king in His own parable going "with ten thousand to meet him that came against Him with twenty thousand." The conflict between man and Satan was not an even match. And our Lord was to overcome, not as God ("for God cannot be tempted with evil")—though He never ceased to be God—but as man. If ever we see Him laying aside His divine prerogatives, it is here. He was to conquer in that unequal fight, and we may well believe that He was specially prepared for it. The text tells us that the time and place were not of Satan's choosing. "Then (and not before) was Jesus led up of the Spirit (*i.e.,* the Holy Spirit which came upon Him at His baptism) into the wilderness to be tempted of the devil."

This may serve to remind us that the devil is not almighty. He cannot go where he will, to attack whom he will. As he said to Jehovah concerning His servant Job "Hast not thou made an hedge about him," so might he have said, perhaps, concerning the Lord Jesus. There had been a hedge about Him during those thirty years at Nazareth, so that He could not be dragged forth before the world, or drawn into special conflict, before His hour was come.

This also serves to remind us of our Lord's true humanity. God caused Him to grow in grace, as well as in wisdom and stature, until He attained His full strength, before He allowed Him to be "led by the Spirit into the wilderness to be tempted of the devil."

Of the first forty days of temptation we know nothing. During those days our Lord fasted. "He did eat nothing" and "He was with the wild beasts." With what He was occupied we do not know. Did He see the pattern of His lifework spread out before Him, the temple that He must build of Jew and Gentile, and the glory that He must

IN THE WILDERNESS

bear, together with the cost of laying its foundation in the ransom of souls, as Moses saw the pattern of the tabernacle during the first forty days when he fasted in Horeb.?Or, like Moses during his second fast of forty days, did our Lord spend His time in prayer and supplication, laying the sins and weakness of His people before His God? Or did both of these occupations fill His thoughts?

Were these the pursuits in which He was continually interrupted by the temptations of the devil, or by the voice of the roaring lions "that came up from the swelling of Jordan," seeking whom they might devour?

We cannot say. And yet it is hardly likely that our Lord began that wonderful work for our redemption without some plan spread out before Him, some revelation to His human spirit of what its design was to be. But however these days were passed, they were at length concluded. The supernatural communion with God, that sustained even the body without nourishment, was over. When the days were ended, He afterwards hungered. And the Christ being now free from that which before had occupied Him, the tempter drew near and claimed His entire attention. Beginning with that which lay nearest to the surface, he suggested that our Saviour should supply His bodily wants. "If Thou be the Son of God, command that these stones be made bread."

Now of course we know that what is suggested by Satan is more likely to be wrong than right. But let us put this question fairly. If we did not know it from the Bible, could we see any harm in this suggestion? The thing looks so entirely innocent. If He was hungry, it was clear that God meant Him to have food. He did not mean Him to die of starvation before His life-work was even begun. The forty days' fast was over. Then why not satisfy His hunger? He had the power to do it undoubtedly. Why trouble others to minister to Him when He could serve Himself? There would be no display about it. Nobody need know. What harm could it do?

Was it not an act of faith to put forth this power and command the stones to change their nature? If faith can remove mountains, why should it be unbelief to turn stones into bread? I do not think that without our Saviour's answer we should have seen the act to be wrong. To me this temptation seems like a searching question on the whole of our Lord's previous life as well as on the principles of that ministry which He had just begun. What manner of man must He have been, who could return this answer and be sure of its right application? "It is written, Man shall not live by bread alone, but by every word that proceedeth out of the mouth of God."

There were to be miracles in His subsequent ministry, but when, and where, and what miracles, God alone must prescribe. Not for Satan, not for self, not for His own mother would He put forth the power that God had given Him until He received orders. That is the great reason for refusing. He will not do this thing without the divine bidding. It was not forbidden, but it was not yet commanded. Miracles are not to be wrought to please man or for the convenience of man: they are exhibitions of Almighty power. They can only be permitted for God's glory at the

IN THE WILDERNESS

express command of God.

It will be found that this principle divides the miracles of the Bible from the miracles of all other religions of the earth. Even where miraculous power is at its height, and the greatest profusion of miracles is about us in Holy Scripture, we are sure to see something which shows that the power is not to be wielded merely for the gratification of the worker, but only at the word of the Lord.

Thus, in the Old Testament, Elisha raised the dead child of the Shunammite to life, but not the husband of the poor widow mentioned in the same chapter (2 Ki. 4), to whom he supplied the oil. "Many lepers were in Israel" in the time of the same prophet, but "none of them was cleansed, saving Naaman the Syrian."

In the New Testament we do not read of one appealing to our Lord in vain for help. That, we may well say, was impossible. "Him that cometh to Me I will in no wise cast out." Yet there must have been many who did not make the appeal. How many times must He have passed that cripple who was carried daily to the beautiful gate of the temple, whom Peter and John set upon his feet at last! If we look closely, we shall see that miracles are quite as conspicuous by their absence, as by their appearance on the sacred page. But this is not obvious at first. We cannot say that it was easy to make the answer to Satan's first onset which our Lord made, that before He wrought a miracle, He must first receive a distinct order from the Author of miraculous power.

I do not pretend to say that this is the whole meaning of His answer, but there is reason for believing it to be the main point. If the answer had not been a real answer, Satan was not likely to take it. If he did not reply to these divine answers, we may be certain he had no reply to make, for he was quite as much in earnest as our Lord.

The next temptation related by Matthew is the temptation in Jerusalem. "Then the devil taketh Him up into the holy city, and setteth Him on the pinnacle (*i.e.,* the highest point) of the temple (probably a high tower over the Eastern entrance, overhanging the steep valley beneath), and saith unto Him, If thou be the Son of God, cast Thyself down from hence" (as Luke adds) *i.e.,* not in the wilderness, but in the sight of all Jerusalem, that men may see Thee descending from on high, for "It is written, He shall give His angels charge over Thee, to keep Thee" (Luke again), and (*i.e.,* It is also written) "In their hands they shall bear Thee up, lest at any time Thou dash Thy foot against a stone."

On this temptation much discussion has been raised. In what sense are we to understand it? Was Satan permitted to take our Lord bodily to Jerusalem and set Him visibly on that giddy height and then propose the leap to the ground? Or was He taken to Jerusalem in the spirit, like the prophet Ezekiel, who went thither in the visions of God from among the captives by the river of Chebar?

On this matter, perhaps, we can never be fully informed in this world, nor can we expect all men to agree. The temptation was real. We may compare what Paul says "I know a man (not I knew, but) I know a man in Christ…whether in the body I cannot tell; or whether out of the body, I cannot tell: (God knoweth), such an one caught up to the third heaven" (2 Cor. 12). The thing happened to Paul. It was real. The revelation remained with him. He knew the unspeakable words which it was not lawful for man to utter. But how he came to know them, he knew not. All he could say, was "I know."

Returning to the story of the temptation, we must remember that our Lord Himself is the only possible authority for this narrative. There were no witnesses. As Christ told His disciples, so they have told us. It really happened therefore, but how, we cannot tell. God knows.

Upon the pinnacle of the temple, then, our Lord stood supported by the enemy, for it was he who took Him there. He then suggested that our Lord should cast Himself down. It may well occur to us that there was in this position no slight cruelty. Flesh and blood, of which our Lord was partaker, would not easily endure the situation with calmness. To one in the body it must have been terrible. To one out of the body even more intensely real. To stand in the grasp of Satan where there is but a step between man and death!

And then, as Jesus had signified His intention of acting under orders in obedience to the written Word, the Word itself is cited by the tempter. "Cast Thyself down from hence" for some such thing as I propose has been foretold of Thee. "For it is written, He shall give His angels charge over Thee, to keep Thee" (keep Thee continually), and "in their hands they shall bear Thee up, lest at any time Thou dash Thy foot against a stone."

The words are written in Psalm 91. They are not misquoted as some say, for if we look closely at the original in Luke, we may see that it is not a single quotation with a few words omitted, but a double quotation of two sentences lying near each other in the same Psalm. "It is written that He shall give..." and that "In their hands..." These words are applied by the tempter to our Lord. He does not deny the application. If they apply to Him we may ask, "When were they fulfilled?" We do not know. Satan suggested that they might be fulfilled in a miracle, which would not only release Him from that horrible situation, but would at once convince the people at Jerusalem that He was their Messiah and their King.

It was a wonderful temptation! To be held in the arms of the evil one on that dizzy height, to feel as unsafe as man could feel, in the hands of His bitterest enemy, and to be told to cast Himself from thence into the arms of the angels, relying on His heavenly Father's written word!

And this second temptation is couched in the very spirit of our Lord's answer to the first. He would trust God with His life. Well, let Him do it. Surely it were better than to trust Satan. One would prefer to escape his hands at all events, if there were nothing else to support one above the abyss. What a temptation it was! And again we must add, What an answer! If My heavenly Father should leave Me in the arms of Satan, shall I not trust Myself there? Shall I cast Myself down without His orders at Satan's bidding, even to escape Satan himself. No! He would not do it, though it passes human wisdom to say how He detected the fact that this passage of the Psalmist did not apply.

I believe the thing that saved Him, humanly speaking,

IN THE WILDERNESS

was the same principle as before. The leap from the pinnacle was not commanded. And we may learn something more from our Lord's answer, "It is written again, Thou shalt not tempt the Lord thy God."

If we verify this reference we find the words run thus, "Ye shall not tempt the Lord thy God, as ye tempted Him in Massah" (Deut. 6:16). How did they tempt Him in Massah? In Exodus 17 it says, "Because they tempted the Lord, saying, 'Is the Lord among us, or not?'" Apply this to our Saviour's position in the arms of Satan on the pinnacle of the temple. "Where is now Thy God? Is Thy God with Thee or not?"

Satan suggested by his seizure of our Lord's person that God could not be with Him. "Rather He has given Thee over to me, the wicked one. Cast Thyself out of my arms into His and those of His faithful angels." But not so our Lord. He had faith to believe that His Father could support Him even in Satan's arms.

It was not necessary to hurl Himself thence. The angels could protect Him there, as well as in falling. If they could preserve Him while He fell, could they not also protect Him where He stood? Thus did He expose the subtle suggestion of the wicked one, that God had forsaken His beloved Son. He had not forsaken Him. He had not prescribed a miraculous leap from the temple any more than He had ordered the turning of the stones into bread. Had Satan dared to hurl Him whom he tempted from the pinnacle, no doubt the angels were at hand. But he dared not do it. And certainly our Lord would not do so Himself, either to escape the horror of Satan's presence and the indignity of being under his protection, or to excite the wonder of the Jews. He would not tempt His God by doubting His presence even there.

Suicide can never be a proof of faith in God. Is it not rather presumptuous unbelief, for "He is not a God of the dead, but of the living." Where, then, is the advantage of throwing away one's life? It is but "tempting Him in Massah. Is the Lord among us or not?"

Time will not permit us to pursue this subject further. The lines of thought that run through this scene are endless. But let us at least seize one grand principle in the example of our Lord. We see how He succeeded where every other man has failed. He detected the evil principle in Satan's suggestions, where all seemed plausible and good. But I think the most striking feature is His refusal to act without express orders. As soon as human intelligence begins to discuss what is right, without reference to Jehovah, sin necessarily begins.

It was sin for Eve to discuss with the tempter the question of eating of the tree of knowledge. God made man to be like Himself. This he cannot be without knowing His will. And God's will cannot be known by a creature without the teaching and guidance of God. Our Lord looked for this in all His actions. "I do always those things that please Him." The lesson for us? Not to move in matters of right and wrong without divine guidance. God has promised the Holy Spirit to those that ask Him. So there is no excuse for moving without His word.

Let us also remember that our Lord is not only our example in resisting temptation. The devil whom the dis-

IN THE WILDERNESS

ciples could not move, departed in obedience to our Lord's majesty. Yet He said, "This kind goeth not out but by prayer and fasting." He did not send them to fast and pray, but gave deliverance Himself. So He will do to us. The victory wherewith we are to overcome, is the victory that He gives. The life that He imparts is the life of the second Man, the risen, victorious, glorified Lord. When He met Satan, He met an enemy before whom no man had yet been able to stand.

When we meet Satan, we meet a beaten foe. And this thought is not to make us despise our enemy, but rather to draw us nearer to our Lord. He has given us the command to pray, "Lead us not into temptation." He has promised to bruise Satan under our feet. Let us lay hold of the promise and resist the devil, looking for the way of escape to Christ, and he will flee from us.

CHAPTER EIGHT

THE THIRD TEMPTATION

Again, the devil taketh Him up into an exceeding high mountain, and showeth Him all the kingdoms of the world, and the glory of them; and saith unto Him, All these things will I give thee, if thou wilt fall down and worship me. Then saith Jesus unto him, Get thee hence, Satan: for it is written, Thou shalt worship the Lord thy God, and Him only shalt thou serve.
MATTHEW 4:8-10

This is the last of the three great temptations with which our Lord was tempted in the wilderness. Luke in his narrative places this second, and the temptation on the pinnacle of the temple in Jerusalem last. He had reasons for this alteration in the order, which we will notice presently. Let us observe first that Matthew professes to relate the three temptations in the order in which they come. Luke does not. Matthew, after the answer to the first temptation, says, "*Then* the devil taketh Him up into the holy city" and in verse 8, "*Again* the devil taketh Him." These words "then" and "again" determine the order to be that which is given here. Luke does not connect either of these two last temptations with the one before it in this way. He merely says, "And the devil, takingh Him up into an high mountain," "and he brought Him to Jerusalem." Matthew and Luke do not contradict each other, for Matthew alone professes to fix the order of the three events. In many other matters, the order of the two Evangelists is different. And there is always a reason for it.

It is evident from the answer given to Satan on the mountain, "Get thee hence, Satan," that this was his last effort. He was dismissed, because he had no more to say. He had tried all his resources, offered all he could command. It was now time for him to depart. The first thing that seems to strike us about this temptation is the change of tone. From doubt Satan now turns to admiration, and from intimidation to flattery. "If Thou be the Son of God," were the opening words of his first and second temptation. But his insinuations had been disregarded. His schemes were exposed, the flaws in his argument laid bare. Our Lord Jesus Christ had shown that He could neither be forced nor frightened into sin. After this the devil admits that he could not deceive or ensnare Him, and gives up the attempt.

He takes our Lord with him into an exceeding high mountain, and employing all his skill as "prince of the power of the air," he produces there a panorama of the kingdoms of the world and all their glories, and makes them float before the eyes of Him who came to win them for Himself. He then says, "I see it is useless any longer

THE THIRD TEMPTATION

to attempt to blind the wisdom of the Son of God. I know what must follow. 'Thou art worthy to receive glory and honor and power' and Thou shalt receive them. Behold, the world is before Thee. Take it. Take all that the god and prince of this world has to offer. It has been delivered to me. When those whom God made to rule it, yielded to my persuasion in Paradise, it fell into my hands. But I will give it all up to Thee, if Thou wilt only acknowledge it as my gift, and do homage to the giver. All this will I give Thee, if Thou wilt fall down and worship me. Only prostrate Thyself before me, and all shall be Thine."

Perhaps this does not seem a very strong temptation when we read it as addressed to Him. But, to judge by our own conduct, it is a kind of temptation quite unnecessarily strong for ourselves. If the thing we should like best on earth is set before us, and some slight concession to evil, i.e., to more worldly motives and principles is required, we do not find it so easy to resist.

A very small part of the whole wealth and glory of the world has such a dazzling and absorbing influence on most of us, that it unsteadies our thoughts, throws our judgment out of balance, and excites our fancy too much to allow any calm consideration at all. This was an offer that Satan would not have made unless he felt that it would be appreciated. It was only when our Lord had shown Himself superior to all temptations affecting His mere personal comfort, that Satan propounded this.

We should note too, that the first thing he offered was power, authority, not wealth or glory. Look at it for a moment from the Christian point of view. Consider power and authority as a means of doing good. If you or I had absolute power throughout the world at this moment, is there no abuse we could put down, no evil or mischievous institution we could sweep away, no useful law or rule that we could make? Look at the many open avenues of temptation that one could close. Think of the schools that might be opened, the messengers of glad tidings that might be sent, the provision that might be made for the needy, and so on. Think of unlimited authority, all the resources of the world, and freedom to use them. Would not the good we could do far outweigh the harm of one act of homage to Satan?

Besides, Satan might add, what ill could come of once falling down before me? You have shown that you are my Master. I cannot deceive you. It is useless for me to tempt you. I will resign my seat in your favor, if you will but acknowledge my gift. The fact that our Lord declined it is one of the weightiest facts in the whole Bible.

Concerning the knowledge of good and evil, there is nothing that goes deeper than this. Here were God and man in one person. God, who can detect all that is not of His own will; and man, acting in the most entire obedience to that which God had willed, met together here, and answered Satan from the written word. "Get thee hence, Satan; for it is written, Thou shalt worship the Lord thy God, and Him only shalt thou serve."

We must remember, too, what this refusal of our Lord draws after it. If He would not take the whole authority of the world from Satan, neither would He take a part of that authority from anyone else.

THE THIRD TEMPTATION

They crucified Him on the pretense that He had tried to do so. The superscription of His accusation was written over, and it was "The king of the Jews." But Pilate, who pronounced the sentence of death, knew well that he condemned Him on a false charge. Our Lord would not commit Himself to the Jews, lest they should force some temporal authority upon Him. He would not permit them to make Him king. He would not cooperate with their plans for obtaining worldly power. And it was this which really brought Him to His end, as far as the Jews were concerned. He would make no league with the powers of this world, and therefore they felt compelled to do away with Him. He claimed divine authority, while He refused to wield human authority. He established a power on earth to which all authority must one day bend. Men did not understand this (do they understand it now?), and instinctively they felt themselves under the necessity of crucifying "the Lord of glory." Caiaphas expressed it in plain words. Pilate gave in to Jewish importunity.

As the Master was treated, so has His church been treated. First, Satan attempted to starve and destroy it; when he failed through that tactic, he tried to corrupt it by the gift of worldly power, with some measure of success.

In this third temptation, our Lord has been separated from us more entirely than in any other. A Christian man cannot always refuse temporal authority as our Lord refused it. But how hard it has been for Christians to hold authority in this world, without giving up, more or less, the strict principles of the law of Christ, and more or less admitting the supremacy of the evil one! It is a very difficult subject on which we have now entered, and perhaps we have gone as far on this line as is profitable.

Let me now endeavor to gather up some of the "fragments that remain." Luke, by putting this temptation before the one in Jerusalem, has reminded us of two things. First, of the temptation in Paradise. There "the woman saw that the tree was (1) good for food," (2) "pleasant to the eyes," like this offer of the world's glory, and (3) "a tree to be desired to make one wise," like the miraculous escape from Satan, on the pinnacle of the temple, the false display of which was to be made a sign to the Jews.

He has also reminded us by his arrangement of the three temptations that the second temptation was addressed to our Lord, as Son of David, while that upon the mountain appealed to Him as Son of Man and Saviour of the world.

John has also presented the three temptations to us in Luke's order, where he speaks of "the lust of the flesh, and the lust of the eyes, and the pride of life," as things "not of the Father, but is of the world," which "passeth away and the lust thereof."

The arrangement in Matthew shows the three temptations as addressed to the body, soul, and spirit. We may also find it profitable to notice that all three temptations have a general reference to our Lord's mission, and to the use of His miraculous powers. I would not allow for a moment that these temptations can be explained in the way one writer has explained them—as questions which addressed themselves to the mind of our Saviour upon

THE THIRD TEMPTATION

His discovery that He could work miracles. But certainly these temptations do raise a question which affected His whole ministry. Now that He was to work miracles, of what kind should they be? Had He turned stones to bread to satisfy His own hunger, what reason could there be why He should not satisfy all the bodily wants of Himself and His disciples at their request and at His own will? The world would have gone after Him at once if He had.

Or if He had thrown Himself from the pinnacle and descended to the ground unhurt to amaze the Jews, on what ground could He have refused them any kind of sign or wonder that they might have desired?

"Show a miracle" would have been a frequent request. All the world might easily have been convinced of His power by means of wonders, and might have bowed before Him with unchanged hearts. But we see at once that this would not have served His purpose in coming into the world. And what was that purpose? "Thou shalt call His name Jesus: for He shall save His people from their sins." The object of the temptations of the devil, *i.e.,* the devil's object, is to draw men into sin. But Christ came to be "in all points tempted like as we are" to be tempted, and not to sin. And therefore nothing except what would lead to this end was profitable for our Saviour. The object of His coming was to destroy the works of the devil, to make it possible that men should be without sin.

It would have been of no use to draw the world to the feet of a Saviour who could not show them the way not to sin. And He, by His life and death for us, admitted that in our fallen nature—in the world as ruled by Satan—to restore sinlessness is not possible. Therefore He chose the cross and not the throne. Therefore He refused this world's authority, and laid down His natural life, that He might become a second man, another Adam, the founder of a sinless race of men, women and children, who should be born again into God's image, and grow up after His likeness for evermore.

And now let me return, in conclusion, to the words, "He was in all points tempted like as we are, yet without sin." When we are tempted, we do not enter into the conflict, as He did in the first instance, without sin.

To tempt the sinless is one thing. He may resist, and be sinless still. To tempt the sinner is another thing. He begins under a disadvantage. He may overcome, but he is a sinner still. And at any time, Satan can bring against him what he could never bring against our Saviour, the fact and the weight, and perhaps the habit, of former personal sin.

Well, I know that difficulty. I fully admit it. How can I set it aside? And yet it is a difficulty of which far more is made, both by the tempter when he would discourage us, and by our own hearts, than we need allow, or than the difficulty is worth.

In the first place we may see, as I have already endeavored to point out, that our Lord's temptations were far more grievous and pressing than ours can ever be. "He… suffered being tempted," as no one else has suffered before or since. And no man had ever overcome before Him. He had nothing in which to fight, but that

THE THIRD TEMPTATION

common humanity, which had been Satan's tool and slave for four thousand years before He came. Of the uses to which that enslaved humanity had been accustomed, the names in the first chapter of Matthew may serve to remind us. Look at the sins which descended upon the Son of Joseph by legal inheritance, the sins of the people whom He came to save. Although evil had no place in His nature, yet by imputation this inheritance was His.

Besides that, there is another thing to be known and remembered, which we do not always grasp. The strength of evil habits is represented to us in temptation and by the tempter as a chain impossible to break. Now that is a delusion. The theory of habit partly fails in the case of the Christian because it takes no account of the doctrine of the two natures. A lost soul cannot be accustomed to do good. "That which is born of the flesh is flesh." "Can the Ethiopian change his skin?"

On the other side, a ransomed spirit cannot be accustomed to do evil. "That which is born of the spirit is spirit." "If any man be in Christ," there is new creation. There is a new man inside the old man and both together are alive. What perplexes the Christian is the fact that he is himself a kind of battleground between two natures. Both are in himself, one unable to sin, the other unable to please God. And his life is a mixture of the two. What his old self does is sin, or good done badly and from bad motives. What his new-born spirit does is good, even if the evil nature is expressing itself, and doing and acting after its kind, at the same time.

But the disheartening thought that we have so long

been tied with the chain of sin that we cannot break it, is only a falsehood of Satan's, and a most pernicious lie. The bands of habit can no more bind the power of Christ than the cords that bound Samson. When the spirit of God came upon him, "He brake them from off his arms like a thread." When the Christian overcomes, it is because Christ gives him the victory. It is Christ within who bursts the bonds. The victory is a free gift, not won by labor, but received from Him.

We want more faith to look at Him, who "was made to be sin for us," and crucified for us; and to perceive that our old man, the home of all evil habits, was "crucified with Him, that the body of sin might be destroyed, that henceforth we should not be enslaved to sin."

Practically, the only way to get rid of evil habits, is to crowd them out with good ones. The amount of strength and energy a human being has, is limited. If it is all laid out in the service of God, there is not much left for the devil to work with. Of course he will take advantage of us, like Amalek, who "smote the hindmost," and the feeblest, when Israel was "faint and weary." And we shall cry out, "O, wretched man that I am! who shall deliver me from the body of this death?" As long as we live, the sinful nature, when it arises, is as strong as ever within us, and as sinful as ever. It becomes apparently even more sinful, in proportion as the eye of the soul sees more of the holiness and the glory of God. As long as we live we shall bear about in the body the remains of fallen nature. "That which is born of the flesh, is flesh," and does not change to spirit.

THE THIRD TEMPTATION

But we must also bear about in the body always, "the dying of the Lord Jesus, that the life also of Jesus might be made manifest in our body." We shall never be like our Master, sinless, until we see Him as He is. Were it otherwise, we might perhaps forget that He is the Master, and cease to acknowledge to Him how much we owe. Israel might vaunt themselves and say, "Mine own hand hath saved me." We must be content with His grace and sympathy. We shall find the grace sufficient. The sympathy will never fail.

With regard to particular habits and forms of sin, there are particular deliverances, that come like our Lord's miracles, or like the exploits of the saviours and judges whom He raised up. But these things do not come to everyone every day. And if we feel that our life can reach a higher standard, as indeed it can, there is one way to raise it, and, I believe, only one. That is to be more in communion with the Lord Jesus Christ. More prayer is what we want.

It is not an easy thing to pray. If the statistics of real prayer were published, we should have much cause to be ashamed. But that is the thing we want to learn, to come oftener, and to keep nearer to the throne of grace, to pray not merely in temptation, but beforehand against temptation, that those things which are occasions of sin may not be permitted to become so to us.

Remember our Lord's constant praying. I have more than once been struck with the way in which experienced Christians make a special point of asking in their morning prayers, that they may be kept from surprises and occasions of sin throughout the day. It is more than half the battle not to be taken unprepared. It is far easier to stop temptation beforehand, than when the hour is come. Let us not be ashamed of admitting to ourselves what is certainly true, that it is not at all a common thing, or an easy thing, to pray. Let us ask our Lord to teach us how to do it, and try to do it more. We shall fight much better if we do. But when we have done it all, the glory of the victory will be our Saviour's. "Not unto us, O Lord, not unto us, but unto Thy name give glory."

"To him that overcometh," will I give this, and this, He says. But what shall we give to Him? To Him who won the victory, to Him who has the salvation in His own hand? Might He not well say, "Ye call Me the Master and the Lord: and ye say well; for so I am." Oh, how can any man not love the Lord Jesus Christ? God give us grace to love Him more.

CHAPTER NINE

JUST AND HAVING SALVATION

Rejoice greatly, O daughter of Zion; shout, O daughter of Jerusalem: behold, thy King cometh unto thee: He is just, and having salvation; lowly, and riding upon an ass, and upon a colt the foal of an ass.
ZECHARIAH 9:9

There are some subjects which it seems hardly possible to contemplate without getting lost in a maze of wonder. And this subject is the greatest of them all. If we turn over the gospel narrative and see what belongs to the seven days commonly called Passion Week, we are bewildered with it all.

There is the entry of our Lord into Jerusalem from Bethany, amidst the Hosannas of the disciples. "Save now, I beseech Thee," was their cry to Him who was "just and having salvation." But they knew not what they asked. Could the children have cried Hosanna if they had known that He could not save them unless He died upon the cross?

There is this entry into Jerusalem that is so full of

meaning; and the tears of the Saviour over the city that He could not save.

On the Monday, He cleansed the Temple and drove the buyers and sellers for the last time from His Father's house. On the way to Jerusalem that morning, He was hungry and pronounced sentence on the fig-tree that mocked His hunger by showing nothing but leaves.

The Tuesday is the last day of His public ministry, the day that the Evangelists tell us most about. On the morning of that day, the fig-tree was discovered "dried up from the roots." In the afternoon He left the Temple with those solemn words, "Behold, your house is left unto you desolate." And then on the Mount of Olives He foretold "the signs of His coming, and of the end of the world." On that day the Greeks desired to see Him. On that day the voice from heaven, for the third time in His ministry, acknowledged Him as the Beloved of God.

The day's discourse in the Temple was interrupted by evil questionings, queries about His authority, the tribute money, about the resurrection, about the commandments. And there was one unanswerable question on His part, "What think ye of the Christ? Whose Son is He?" On that day He pronounced those solemn woes against the "scribes and Pharisees, hypocrites," despised the heartless liberality of the rich, and acknowledged the generosity of the poor widow.

Who that reads the long story of that day's varied labor and its many calm utterances of heavenly wisdom, would suppose that it was the last day when Jerusalem should hear that voice, and that the Speaker knew all that was to come? And what a wonderful close to that day's utterances is the prophecy of the end of all things, "When the Son of Man shall come in His glory" and "before Him shall be gathered all nations" and everlasting punishment and life eternal shall be the final balancing of the books?

The Wednesday of this week seems to have been spent in retirement at Bethany, marked by nothing except the distinct notice of His immediate betrayal which our Lord gave to His disciples, and the fact that this quiet day gave Judas his opportunity to steal away and make final arrangement with the chief priests.

On Thursday, Peter and John were sent to prepare the Passover. On that evening the Master reentered Jerusalem with the twelve, to sleep no more until all was finished. Loving words and acts were prolonged until the night was come. And then there was Gethsemane and the beginning of the end. That night of fear and treachery and insult at last faded into the dawn of Friday, that brought our Lord face to face with Pilate, and sent Him upon the way of the cross.

Over that cross hangs the veil of thick darkness. But at eventime there is light when all is finished. And the Light of the world (that the cross had seemed to darken), breaks into the darkness of the grave.

On Saturday (the last Sabbath of the unredeemed world), the enemies confess their fear of the Resurrection, and by this dread of Him whom they call "deceiver," admit that they themselves have been deceived. And to make quite sure of the Resurrection, they post their guards to watch for the dawn of Easter day.

To all this week's labor our King came to Jerusalem as on this day. "Behold thy King cometh unto thee," it is written. Have we ever grasped the bare circumstances, the outside facts of this week's toil and suffering, of which no man understood the purpose, not even those who saw it pass before their eyes?

They "trusted that it had been He which should have redeemed Israel," and so they rejoiced greatly when He came to them. But when the work was done, they mourned and wept over it. What He did they knew not at the moment. Afterwards they found out that He loved them and had come to "wash them from their sins in His own blood."

It would be easy enough to lose ourselves in the mere circumstances and just to watch the movements of our Lord and Master through this last week of His ministry, awed and moved by His words and actions, and yet grasping nothing of His purpose all the while. It is something to gaze and worship, if that can deepen our affection and awake our love. But there is more than this for us to do.

One word in our text demands special attention and contains the key to all the rest. That word is "salvation." "He is just, and having salvation." What does this mean? There is a singular beauty in the phrase as it now stands in our English Bible. It is not a common one; it is a single word in the original, and means, not saving others, but "saved." It is the same word in Deuteronomy 33:29, "Happy art thou, O Israel: who is like unto thee, O people *saved* by the Lord?" The word does not mean saving others, but saved.

JUST & HAVING SALVATION

Now in what sense can it be said of our Lord that He was saved? In one sense, of course, it cannot be said, as His enemies well perceived when He hung upon the cross. "He saved others; Himself He cannot save." "If Thou be the Christ, save Thyself and us," said the crucified robber beside Him. Not so. Not by coming down from the cross did He save them. "Having salvation" in His hand, He held it fast, and there He hung and did not let it go.

But in another sense He was saved. We are taught that in Gethsemane, "He had offered up prayers and supplications with strong crying and tears unto Him that was able to save Him from death, and was heard in that He feared."

We read, too, that "He entered in once into the Holy Place, having obtained *(i.e. found)* eternal redemption." "Being made perfect through sufferings, He became the Author of eternal salvation unto all them that obey Him," a well of salvation inexhaustible by the uttermost needs of all that come to God. Look at Him as God, and He is our Saviour. Look at Him as the Son of Man, and He is saved—a man saved from the burden of iniquity and from the tyranny of Satan; delivered *to* the power of darkness, and again delivered *from* the power of darkness; "able also to save them to the uttermost" for evermore.

Is there not a wonderful beauty in those words, "having salvation?" Having it in Himself, and for Himself not using it; having it and keeping it for all who love Him—an inexhaustible store of strength, of victory, of mercy. Having saved thousands upon thousands, and having no less salvation still; so that "If any man sin, we have an advocate with the Father, Jesus Christ the righteous." "Righteous and having salvation;" having it, as one who sits in the life-boat in the midst of the raging ocean, ready to save all that come. Having it, as one whose house is on the rock above the rushing river, saving and sheltering all that are within reach of His hand. Safe Himself, and supporting with His everlasting arms all that will trust themselves to Him. There is a wonderful wealth of safety in these precious words, "Behold thy King cometh unto thee, just and having salvation!"

Of all things that He came to do this week in Jerusalem, the greatest marvel of salvation is His death. I wonder how far we have realized the full meaning of that expression, "Christ died for us." To understand it, if possible, is a step to the understanding of salvation. What does it mean when I say, "He died for me" What is it that is accomplished, from the sinner's point of view?

Speaking of myself as a fallen sinful child of Adam, I am in this dilemma. I want to die, and I want to live. And I can do neither. I want to die because I am like one who is incurably diseased. My "heart is deceitful above all things, and desperately wicked"—so sinful that I feel it to be past all cure. I want to die to sin, that I may be rid of the pain of sinning. Many a one who does not grieve for the disobedience of sin, would gladly be rid of the pain of sinning. And some would like to be rid of both. But how can we? To part with the body of sin is not necessarily to part with sin itself. It might only end in the everlasting exclusion of the soul and spirit from the presence of God our Maker, and in what state?

As to that, "the sinners in Zion are afraid." "Who among us shall dwell with the devouring fire? Who among us shall dwell with everlasting burnings?" If that is the place where lost ones are consigned, I cannot face that death. And yet I want to die that I may be rid of my sin; for I feel that my sinful heart is incurable while this life lasts.

And if I want to die, how much more would I desire to live! If the sick man's sickness is so sore that he would rather die than turn and toss any longer on his bed of pain and weariness, ask him what be would give to rise from it in renewed health and perpetual vigor!

It is almost too good to wish for. Fallen man has become so used to his state of sickness that he can say to inquirers most days, "I am quite well, thank you." How long is it since any man stood on earth who could truly say, "I am quite well?" I want to die and cannot. But what if, instead of dying, I could live? "When we were yet without strength," not strong enough to die and far too weak to live, "in due time Christ died for the ungodly."

He died the death that we could not die—laid down the soul that He received by birth, as men take off and lay aside a garment—laid it down through the power of the Creator, without facing the "everlasting burnings."

And He so laid it down that He might take it up again by new creation. "Raised up from the dead by the glory of the Father," He awoke to "newness of life," to "an inheritance incorruptible, and undefiled, and that fadeth not away," a state wherein "the inhabitant shall not say, I am sick." And having done this in our place, dying as we could not die, and rising from whence we could not rise, He invites us to be partakers of His divine nature, to be crucified with Him, buried with Him, risen with Him, ascended with Him, to live a life hidden with Him now, which shall be revealed hereafter. Such salvation as this our King came to bring us.

There is no earthly illustration that will explain it. The innocent man cannot die for the murderer among men. If both were willing, mankind would not permit it. For the murderer would still live, and society would not be secure. To die for sinful man so that man should not die, and so that the sinner and the sin should die, and to deal justly with the interests of all concerned—this was the problem of our salvation, the problem solved by our King. "He is just and having salvation;" though He died, "the just for the unjust," and is still undefiled—our "advocate with the Father, Jesus Christ the righteous," "the propitiation...for the sins of the whole world."

I have only time to touch on one other topic in the text. And that is the practical one, the dominion over the hearts of men which our King and Saviour came to take. Both ends of our text betoken it. "Rejoice greatly, O daughter of Zion." None but those who are loyal can rejoice at the coming of the King. And the imagery with which His coming was attended betokens it also.

Why is so much made of the fact that He entered Jerusalem "riding on an ass"? Why not rather "in a chariot of fire with horses of fire;" or, like the Queen of Sheba "with a very great train, with camels" or as in the book of Revelation, upon "a white horse," with a bow and a crown, "conquering, and to conquer"?

The text directs attention to His lowliness—"lowly, and riding upon an ass." And so indeed it may appear to us. But not so much so to His followers at that time. His Majesty rather than His lowliness was the thing men noticed then. "When He was come into Jerusalem, all the city was moved, saying, Who is this?" The lowliness is in Himself rather than in His surroundings. The ass upon which He rode is the chosen symbol for man. "Man be born like a wild ass's colt."

Concerning the ass's colt, the law had spoken expressly: "Every firstling of an ass thou shalt redeem with a lamb." It was the untamed, unredeemed savagery and wilfulness of human nature that our King came to win over and subdue at this time. And it is noticeable that both Jew and Gentile were brought to Him in a figure here. Matthew tells us that He sent for "an ass tied and a colt with her;" one that had borne the yoke and one that had not. Matthew leaves it quite uncertain upon which of the two He was to ride. Mark, Luke, and John mention the colt only. "A colt tied whereon yet never man sat," was what He asked for. And He rode thereon. And John, who, like Matthew, cites the prophecy, even omits the mention of the ass from the Old Testament quotation, and only regards the colt. It may well serve to indicate what was in the first days of the gospel not quite certain, that the Jewish nation who had borne the yoke of the law, would refuse to have Jesus as their Master. The Gentiles who had never known God's yoke, accepted the Lord Jesus gladly as their King.

SHADOWS OF REDEMPTION

Matthew, writing early, leaves the question as it were open; the other three evangelists treat it as a settled thing. And yet John, who wrote last of all, gives, I believe, a remarkable hint in his way of citing the prophecy, that he foresaw the day when Jew and Gentile together would acknowledge Jesus as their Lord. If you turn to John 12:15, you will see he writes our text with a variation, "Fear not, daughter of Zion." "Fear not," instead of "Rejoice greatly." And why "Fear not?" Because before the end of his life, something had happened to Zion which might well cause fear, lest the Lord had forsaken her and her God had forgotten her.

I suspect that John in this verse has not simply given the sense of our text, but has combined it with a portion of another, as he and other New Testament writers often do. Look at Zephaniah 3:14 you will find a similar passage, "Sing, O daughter of Zion," etc. "The King of Israel, even the Lord, is in the midst of thee...In that day it shall be said to Jerusalem, Fear thou not, and to Zion, Let not thine hands be slack. The Lord thy God in the midst of thee is mighty; He will save."

But these are but the circumstances and the imagery with which the truth is embellished. For each of us the word of the text is, "Behold thy King cometh unto thee." How shall we receive Him? He comes to claim dominion over our wilful hearts. Our wilfulness has brought us into deep need of salvation. "He is just and having salvation." Shall we bow down our wilful hearts before Him and say, "I am Thine, O save me. I have gone astray like a lost sheep," or rather like "a wild ass used to the wilderness," seeking anything rather than divine control? But O "seek Thy servant" and "grant us Thy salvation," and subdue my iniquities; for Thou, O Lord Jesus, didst "come to seek and to save that which was lost."

CHAPTER TEN

STRANGER IN JERUSALEM

And the one of them, whose name was Cleopas, answering said unto Him, Art thou only a stranger in Jerusalem, and hast not known the things which are come to pass there in these days?
LUKE 24:18

It is not unreasonable to ask this question on the third day after our Lord's death. The things "concerning Jesus of Nazareth, which was a prophet mighty in deed and word before God and all the people; and how the chief priests and rulers there delivered Him to be condemned to death and have crucified Him,"—these things were sufficiently remarkable, even apart from the expectation that it might be He who "shall redeem Israel." Even a solitary stranger in the Holy City would scarcely fail to know what was done. And if it was so then, how is the case now? Not only in Jerusalem, but "from the one side of heaven unto the other," the fame of those things that were done in Jerusalem has spread. In every nation under heaven, I suppose, there are some persons who know that these things were done for them—that Jesus of Nazareth was crucified for their sakes.

From the narrative of the four Gospels, an attentive reader may obtain a fuller and clearer view of what was done to Jesus than could have been obtained by many an eye-witness at the time. The view of an eye-witness is but one view, and that a partial one. He cannot be everywhere, or see all that passes, in so great a transaction as this. There was not any one person except our Lord Himself, who saw all that we may read of what He suffered, from His betrayal to His grave.

For instance, the private compact of Judas, and the message to Pilate from his wife, and other things which we might mention, must have been unknown to many until the time was past. But now all has come to light. We moreover know the reason for the death of our Saviour, which was hidden from many who saw Him die. And thus our view is better than theirs.

But I feel as if the question of the text might be asked of many, with good reason. I know it might be asked of me, "Art thou only a stranger in Jerusalem, and hast not known the things which are come to pass there in these days?" And I must answer, as our Lord did, but for a different reason, "What things" or, as it is more exactly, "What kind of things?" There is something here that I want to know, of which I feel that I have very little grasp. Let me endeavor to explain my meaning, that we may together approach the inquiry which our text suggests.

We all know and confess thus much, that "Christ died for our sins according to the Scriptures." We believe that, without the shedding of His blood, for us there is no forgiveness; but that "in Him we have redemption through His blood, even the forgiveness of our sins." We give thanks "unto Him that loved us, and washed us from our sins in His own blood" for "the innumerable benefits, which by His precious blood-shedding, He hath obtained to us."

But I cannot bring myself to speak only of the benefits of Christ's death for us on the day on which He died. If a friend of mine had secured some considerable inheritance for me, and saved my life at the expense of his own, I should not choose the anniversary of his death to feast and rejoice in my inheritance. Every day besides in the whole year I might do that. But that one day, the joy would be sobered by the recollection of the life laid down. I could almost put my inheritance and its blessings and comforts from me and wish myself poor again, if the life that redeemed me might have been spared. I am sure you will all enter into this feeling. And have we not some reason today for going in spirit to Jerusalem, and asking ourselves, whether we know the things that were done in that city as on this day.

We have some notion of the dreary catalogue of sorrows and indignities which our Friend, "the Friend of sinners," endured before He died. There was the slow treachery of Judas, which He saw gradually working to its conclusion before His eyes. There was the gradual approach of the last conflict, and the enemy that held his strength in reserve till then. The repeated trials before several different tribunals, the injustice and cruelty increasing at every step. First Annas, then Caiaphas and the council, and then Pilate and Herod, and Pilate again; the constant ill-usage by so many sets of tormentors, with but one weary victim to bear the malice of them all; the cruel mocking and scourging, and at last the nails and the torture of the cross. This long dreary list of miseries we read over again and again, and are inclined to turn away from it. It is horrible to think that it should grow familiar in the reading; and yet it would be almost impossible to realize it and to read it at the same time.

And what was it all for? Supposing that we understand the necessity of our Saviour's death, seeing that sinful man must die—supposing that we see the justice of God on the one side, and His love upon the other, and believe in the marvelous wisdom by which He has set both before us in the death of His Son—yet is there not this other question besides, rising up in the heart at such a time as this, and crying aloud for satisfaction? Granted that our Saviour must die, yet what was the necessity for all this load of suffering, heaped and accumulated upon Him for so many hours before His death, from the time that He sat down to supper with the traitor, and was seized with sorrow at the thought of such horrible wickedness drawing nearer and nearer to one of His own chosen disciples, until the last loud cry that He uttered upon the cross? If His blood was the penalty of our sins, yet why should that penalty have been exacted in such a fearful way? Is it part of the doom of sinful souls to be tortured as well as to die? Was all the anguish that is caused by treachery and coldness and desertion and injustice (repeated in every possible form under the cover of the law) and falsehood and insult and mockery, to say nothing of brutality and downright violence of the most ferocious kind—was all this as essential to our salvation, as the one great fact which is selected as the foundation of doctrine in the midst of it all, that the precious blood of Christ shed was the ransom for our souls?

When we sit down to meditate quietly on these things, what can we say? For my part, I feel a stranger in Jerusalem indeed. "I cannot but know the things that came to pass there in these days." But still the question that Jesus asked His disciples is before me, "What kind of things?" It may be foolish and "slow of heart" not to see, in all the Scriptures, the truth that the Christ was to suffer. That is manifest. Messiah was to be "cut off, but not for Himself." Yet still we ask, what is the cause of all the many details of suffering, which we read at this time, which must be present to the memory of every Christian and be like a silent burden on his heart? If Christ must die for us, of necessity, why must His sufferings be so tremendous, so intolerable, so protracted, before He died?

If we cannot at once face the question, perhaps we may at least observe in some measure how it came to be. How was it brought about that our Saviour suffered so bitterly in all these things?

In the first place, we have to remember His nature. He was a sinless man in the midst of sinners. And what does that mean? A man whose feelings and powers and faculties were perfect in the first instance, and had been developed to the highest degree of quickness by proper use, never dulled or perverted or misapplied in any way so as to deaden them. Our Saviour was not only "the Life" in respect of His Godhead, but full of life in His manhood. He was most intensely alive. In Him there was no natural tendency to dullness and heaviness, and faintness and decay and death. He died, not so much because they slew Him, but because "He laid down His life."

In our Saviour's own person, there was the highest possible capacity for feeling, and appreciating, and perceiving everything done to Him or around Him, which His bodily senses could convey to His human soul. One cause, therefore, of the greatness of His sufferings was His unusual capacity to feel.

But this is not by any means all that we want to know. This is what enabled our Lord to suffer so much. We have still to ask what it was that *inflicted* so much suffering upon Him. How came Judas to betray Him, and Peter to deny Him, and His other disciples to forsake Him as they did? How came the Jews and their rulers to conceive such enmity against Him that they could deliberately plan to put Him to death? How were so many false witnesses found to offer testimony against Him? Why was He not rescued? Why was Pilate so over-awed by the clamorous multitude that he gave way? And then what incited the servants and the soldiers to all the spiteful mockery, and contempt, and useless cruelty that they practiced upon Jesus Christ? We do not read that they so treated the two thieves who were condemned to the same cruel death. Why then did they so misuse Him who had "done nothing amiss?"

Granting that our sins deserved it all, which they certainly do, how were men persuaded to inflict so many useless, purposeless cruelties upon Him, who did them good and not evil all the days of His life?

There is only one way of answering this question, and a terrible way it is. We can take the individual persons who were concerned in the persecution of our Lord, and follow them, one by one, and point out how they only did very much what other men have been seen to do under similar circumstances; what we can suppose men are capable of doing now, if they met with the same inducement, or were pressured in the same sort of way.

Take the case of Judas. He was invited by the Lord Jesus to follow Him. He did so. He heard His words and saw His wonderful works. He was engaged, we suppose, in preaching for Him sometimes, in waiting upon Him, in bringing into His presence those who came to Him, in receiving money for Him, and probably also in laying out and giving it to the poor. With all this service, he still retained a secret sin, the sin of covetousness. While he waited on his Master, he also helped himself. His heart was set on his own advancement, if he could find an opportunity. And he did find opportunity to rob their common purse. Oh, how terribly easy the road seems now to the same sin!

At last, being provoked by a reproof which our Lord gave him, he was suddenly possessed with the idea that he would bring His enemies upon Him, and, if he could, make some money by the deed. No doubt he hoped to be able to avoid the consequences. Christ would escape by miracle, as He often had done. Judas would obtain the money and would be the better, and no one would be much the worse. He might easily obtain forgiveness from One so ready to forgive. Or if the worst came to the worst, Judas could but leave his Master and be as he was before.

And so he framed and planned his horrible purpose and arranged it with the chief priests. All that was said about the matter at the supper table on that last night still further irritated and vexed him; he went out and did it, very likely under some irritation of temper, and in the morning he saw what he had done. He awoke in the hands of Satan, to find out what a horrible sinner he was. But meantime, that had been accomplished which it was impossible to undo. The first step towards the death of Christ had been taken, a step which it pleased God in His providence that no one should be able to recall.

With this view of Judas, conceive, my brethren, that we hear our Saviour's words repeated, "Verily, verily, I say unto you, that one of you shall betray Me." O how soon the soul is startled into the question, "Lord, is it I?"

From Judas it is not far to the case of Pilate; our Lord Himself put them together when He said before the judgment seat, "He that delivered Me unto thee hath the greater sin." How did Pontius Pilate come to treat our Saviour as he did? Rather, if we regard him as a Roman statesman, what else was he likely to do? Hundreds of thousands of the most turbulent nation in the whole empire were assembled in their chief city at one of the great yearly feasts. For some reason or other they had set their hearts on the death of this prisoner, who had offended their religious scruples in some way. They could make no clear case against Him, but they accused Him of claiming the kingdom, and they threatened Pilate with the vengeance of the Roman Emperor, unless he consented to pass sentence of death. Pilate tried to pacify them, over and over again. But the more he reasoned, the more furious they became. If the prisoner before him were not a criminal, yet surely it was better to sacrifice a single obnoxious person than to run the risk of a rebellion and perhaps a war. It was clear that, whatever Jesus had done, the people hated Him.

What could Pilate do? A very strong governor, sure of his own character, sure of his own position, sure of support from his superiors, and with an overwhelming force at command, might have taken his own way. But such a governor Pontius Pilate was not. A very good man might have risked his own life for the sake of the prisoner. But this might have been lost in a riot. The prisoner might have been killed also, and all authority would have been at an end. Far more enlightened men than Pilate have given way to popular outcry, and done what they knew to be wrong, in much more enlightened countries and in much easier times. And if Pilate gave way at all, he must go the whole length. Nothing short of the death of Jesus of Nazareth was demanded or allowed. Not being a Roman citizen, the prisoner would be crucified, if put to death. If crucified, he would first be scourged; it was only the common custom. The brutality of the soldiers was the cause of all the rest.

Let him that is without covetousness condemn Judas

the betrayer. Let him that never feared the face of man rather than the face of God, condemn Pontius Pilate, who delivered Jesus to the people's will.

And what of the Jewish council? These men were not so much concerned with the death of Christ singly and separately. Their hatred was the opposition of a whole class. We know how it arose in the first instance. It was a mixture of jealousy and religious prejudice, both very strong feelings in the human heart.

In the first instance, they persecuted Jesus because He did miracles on the Sabbath, which, they said, was against Moses' law. Then He rebuked their sinful lives in the plainest language, and claimed divine authority to support His words. They felt His rebukes to be well-deserved, and His accusations true. He put them to silence when they tried to reason with Him, baffled them when they attempted to answer Him. The mass of the people followed Him, and loved Him better than they loved the authorized teachers of the Jewish nation.

Altogether, the Jewish rulers felt their reputation to be shaken and their influence giving way. If they let Him alone, He would soon destroy their position. All men would believe on Him and accept Him as the Son of God. Their influence would be at an end. Here again there could be no compromise. Either Jesus was a blasphemer, or He was the Christ, the Son of the Blessed—a tremendous alternative. They decided to declare Him a blasphemer, and to stop His preaching and His work. Judas gave them an opportunity. They took advantage of it and the thing was done.

Then there is Peter's denial; we need not discuss that. It is the easiest thing to understand, of all the things that were done on that fearful night. But it was another item in the sufferings of our Lord.

There were certain circumstances of His trial which prolonged what He had to endure. It was night when His enemies seized Him. They could not take Him before Pilate until day-break. Meantime, they were detained, idle, and their prisoner was in their power. The very time that hung upon their hands will help to account for the additional insults and cruelties heaped on their prisoner's head.

Besides these persons who were directly and immediately concerned in our Lord's sufferings, how many more there were who were also partly responsible for that which they did not hinder, nor make any effort to prevent. What of all the thousands in Jerusalem? Some were there whom He had healed, many more whom He had fed, and taught, and comforted. All these knew that He had done nothing amiss. Could they have done nothing to prevent His execution if they would? Yet either from indifference, or from lack of energy and vigilance, they attempted nothing, or their attempt came to nothing.

And were they not responsible? Surely they were! Is it not written, "If thou forbear to deliver them that are drawn unto death, and those that are ready to be slain; if thou sayest, Behold, we knew it not; doth not He that pondereth the heart consider it? and He that keepeth thy soul, doth not He know it? and shall not He render to every man according to his works?" Would those who do so little to deliver their fellow creatures in this present time have done more for Jesus Christ?

And now what is all this which produced Christ's prolonged sufferings? What is it all but human sin and weakness—natural man under temptation, doing what pleased him best? If the Saviour is the complete image of holiness, His enemies among them picture every variety of sin. No one person was responsible for it all. It was the work of all together, an astounding combination of circumstances each helping the other out; no one thing by itself so very uncommon, but altogether making the most awful load of suffering that was ever endured.

See what follows. That load of suffering was heaped upon our Saviour, not only for the sake of our sins, but by the operation of our sins. It is we who have sold ourselves to work wickedness, and have so done this deed.

Thus we may see in the death of Christ, as in a mirror, the true image of ourselves. If we open our hearts to the temptations which we see in this picture; if we give way to covetousness, envy, the fear of man, the love of our own ease and the like, what is there to prevent our acting like Judas and Pilate, and the Jews and Peter, if another Jesus of Nazareth were sent among us to show us what we are? Sin will pass more easily in a world of sinners. But when the light of holiness is brought to bear upon it, sin is compelled to discover itself and stand for what it is.

So it was when Christ came into the world. In Him, holiness was offered for man's approval. God, our Maker, came among us, in our own nature, and offered Himself to our friendship and our love. And is it not horrible to think that we should have watched Him, listened to Him, tried Him, and in the end rejected Him, and used Him thus? I say we did it, my brethren, for if the same sin be in us, it is only the lack of opportunity that saves us from the same result. Indifference and self-interest, covetousness and cowardice, envy and treachery, injustice and coarseness and brutality, are just the same things in themselves when there is no Jesus of Nazareth to throw the light of God upon them, as they were when He suffered from them at His death.

Returning to the question of our text, let us each ask it of our own hearts and seek for the true answer. "Art thou," my soul, "only a stranger in Jerusalem, and hast not known the things that are come to pass there in these days?" And if you should answer that question with another, and say, "What kind of things?" then know for sure that these are the very same things that are in your own natural self, and that the pangs of your Saviour's sufferings are only their natural work. Then let us confess to Him, "I have heard of Thee, O my Saviour, by the hearing of the ear, but now mine eye seeth Thee. Wherefore I abhor myself, and repent in dust and ashes."

In that He who suffered for us, accepted all this evil at our hands, and took it meekly and lovingly, giving only good for evil all the while, and sending the message of forgiveness to those who had slain Him from the place where He has gone, we may see that His sufferings were not only the effect of our sins, but the sacrifice which love has made to atone for them, and through which Love itself beseeches us to be "reconciled unto God."

Shall we not ask the pardon which He offers? Shall we not "look upon Him whom we have pierced, and mourn"—and seek for grace to forsake the sin which wounded Him, and caused Him so to die? Thus may we learn the song of those whom He has redeemed, and say, "Unto Him that loved us, and washed us from our sins in His own blood—and He hath made us a kingdom, and priests unto God and His Father; to Him be glory and dominion for ever and ever. Amen."

CHAPTER ELEVEN

SEEN OF ME ALSO

*And last of all He was seen of me also,
as of one born out of due time.*
1 Corinthians 15:8

With these words Paul closes the list of witnesses to the resurrection of our Lord.

The chapter where the text is found deals with the subject in three points of view. There is first the fact of the resurrection affirmed by many witnesses. Next, there is the doctrine of the resurrection as a truth absolutely necessary to the gospel. Thirdly, there is the manner of it, in the case of our Lord and also for those who belong to Him. The chapter may be easily divided under these three heads.

I used to think that I not only believed in the resurrection but also understood it. And now it seems to me that there is nothing in all the gospel of which we understand so little, or on which people think so differently, as the resurrection of the dead. We wonder how the Corinthians, being Christians, could say there was no resurrection. But we must remember that it was not immortality, nor a future life that they denied, nor a judgment after death—things believed by every thoughtful man in the heathen world—but men's resurrection with their bodies. When we ask ourselves how much we know of the difference between living as an angel or spirit, and living in a spiritual body, and why we believe in the one as well as in the other, and yet as a thing distinct from the other, we may perhaps admit after all that the Corinthians were only stating openly and plainly certain doubts and difficulties which are not uncommon, but may easily present themselves to anyone who tries to think clearly about the subject.

Let me try to say a few words on this great wonder in these several points of view. There is (1) the fact, (2) the teaching, (3) the manner of the resurrection. And as we come to each of these in turn, let us ask ourselves how we can lay hold of it.

And first, how do we lay hold of the fact that our Lord did rise from the dead? Paul says to the Corinthians that He delivered to them the fact that Christ rose from the dead as a thing declared by the Old Testament Scriptures and as a thing proved by witnesses. "He rose again the third day according to the Scriptures and…was seen…" Upon the proof that Old Testament prophecy foretold it I cannot now dwell. That is a subject by itself.

But let us look at the testimony of the witnesses. "He was seen." What was seen? Not the resurrection itself. Strange to say, we cannot discover from the New Testament that anyone saw Christ rise from the dead. The

SEEN OF ME ALSO

Roman guards saw an angel of the Lord descend from heaven and "roll back the stone from the door [of the sepulcher] and sit upon it." "For fear of him" those "keepers did shake and became as dead men." The sight was accompanied by an earthquake, which added to its terrors. But we do not read that He who rose from the tomb was seen by them. If they saw Him rise, their names should have stood first on the list of witnesses. But our Lord, on the day of His resurrection and from that time forth, was seen by those to whom He was pleased to show Himself, and not generally by all mankind. He did not appear "to all the people," but to "witnesses chosen before of God," Peter tells us. It is nowhere intimated that the Roman soldiers were among those chosen witnesses.

Further, the mysterious powers of our risen Lord, by which He entered the room where the disciples were assembled with doors bolted, and by which He vanished from the supper table at Emmaus, were quite sufficient to enable Him to leave the tomb unnoticed and invisibly, without disturbing it at all. It was fitting that the sealed and guarded tomb should be opened by an angel to show that His body had not been stolen by the disciples or removed by any human hands, and yet that He was not there. But it was not necessary to open it in order to enable Him to rise. He was not like Lazarus, needing to be loosed by the hands of men, either from the tomb or from the grave clothes. "God raised Him from the dead."

The soldiers then were the only persons (except angels) who can have been present at the resurrection. There is no reason to suppose they saw Christ arise. And if they did not, certainly no other man did. All who came after their departure found an empty tomb. Some saw angels and grave clothes carefully folded. The first who saw Jesus found Him outside the tomb and behind her, while she was stooping to look into the empty grave.

So then, no man saw the resurrection. And if it took place in the same way that the resurrection of Christ's people at His coming is to happen, no one could have watched it, for it must have been done in a moment, in the "twinkling of an eye."

But though no man can have seen Christ rise, many saw Him after He was risen. The women who are mentioned in the Gospels saw Him first. Paul in this place mentions no women (a significant fact in this epistle), but he enumerates the men. "He was seen of Cephas, then of the twelve: After that, He was seen of above five hundred brethren at once, of whom the greater part remain unto this present, but some are fallen asleep. After that, He was seen of James; then of all the apostles. And last of all," says Paul, "He was seen of me." "He was seen" then by all these persons.

Now one thing may be noted concerning all of them. They were all believers in Jesus as the Christ. All were friends of His, none of them enemies. And He was seen by them, not as they saw Him in His earthly life, where they could follow Him and cling to Him and watch His movements; seeing Him and thronging and detaining Him whether He desired their company or not. After His resurrection He was seen when He pleased and by whom He pleased. No one could foretell His coming, or follow

SEEN OF ME ALSO

Him when He went His way. He could not be thronged or pressed by multitudes. He was as much beyond the control of those who saw Him as an angel. He was a being of another world. And even when they saw Him, they did not always recognize Him, unless it was His will to be known. The eyes of the two who went to Emmaus "were holden" for a time, so "that they should not know Him." Certainly those who saw Him were awake and in no trance or vision; but they saw because they were enabled, or at least permitted, to see.

Now this kind of testimony is peculiar. It puts the proof of Christ's resurrection outside the grasp of the unbelieving world. The soldiers of the Roman guard, when they received money to say the body of Jesus had been stolen by His disciples, knew that tale was false. And they might well suspect that the resurrection had taken place, especially if they were not too frightened to examine the empty tomb, as I suspect they were. But they could not prove that "the Lord was risen indeed." The persons who saw the risen Lord were all selected witnesses.

It is clear that an unbeliever might say to this, "Let me choose my witnesses, and I will prove anything you please." So that the world has no present evidence of the resurrection but in the power that the resurrection exercises in the world and through believers' lives. The power of Christianity is the proof to the world that Christ is risen. Men have no other proof until they believe.

And what proof of the resurrection have believers? We can accept the testimony of those who saw the risen Saviour. But the weight of that testimony is according to the meaning and the value that we put upon their words, Paul does not however dwell long on this proof of it. He counts up the witnesses that saw the risen Lord, and then from that fact he passes on to the doctrine. "If Christ be not risen, then is our preaching is vain" and "your faith is vain," and "ye are yet in your sins."

Do you believe in the forgiveness of sins? Then you believe in the resurrection. Do you not believe in the forgiveness of sins? Then you do not believe in the resurrection. You may never have taken the trouble to deny or contradict it, but if it is nothing more to you than a fact in history, it is not a fact at all. If you have ventured nothing upon it, gained nothing by it, learned nothing from it; if you would not suffer anything rather than deny it, it is not true to you. You do not really believe in the resurrection of Christ, however often you may say the Creed.

The resurrection has been called God's "Amen to the death of Christ." "He was delivered for our offenses, and was raised again for our justification." If He had died for us and remained in the grave, He would have secured nothing for us but death. We might have died to sin certainly, and died out of our bodies, and then death would have been the end of the matter. Paul says in plain words, "If Christ be not risen...then they also which are fallen asleep in Christ are perished!" It is to my mind the most touching argument in the whole chapter. "Fallen asleep in Christ" and "perished," lost, undone! Gone from our sight, and gone we know not where! Yet that had been the end of falling asleep in Jesus if He had not risen from the dead. We must have thought of those who are fallen

SEEN OF ME ALSO

asleep in Christ as lost, not gone before; whereas now we can think of them as with Christ in everlasting peace; and when He comes back again, He will bring them back too.

Now we are coming very near to the practical conclusion of this part of our subject. The world has no direct proof of the resurrection. The proof of the resurrection to the church is the sight of the risen Lord.

That sight was given to the apostles to see with their bodily eyes. But even among these witnesses there is a difference. Look at the witness in the text. "Last of all He was seen of me also." And when was He "seen of me?" Not on Easter Day, nor the Lord's day after. Not during all the forty days after His resurrection; not at the moment of His ascension; not for years after that. When then? Suddenly, one day at noon, on the road to Damascus, "a light shone from heaven above the brightness of the sun," and Saul saw the risen Jesus, and heard His voice speaking to Him in His own tongue. That moment He was convinced of the truth that Jesus had risen. He saw Him and heard His voice, and for three days he saw nothing else. "I could not see," he tells us, "for the glory of that light." From that day no one of all Christ's apostles endured so much for His sake. No one preached Him so far and wide. No one saw Him oftener. No one wrote more fully and plainly concerning Him. He saw Him first on the way to Damascus; he saw Him often afterwards in visions, at Jerusalem, and in Paradise, and elsewhere.

He never knew Christ after the flesh. But he knew the risen Christ as well as it is possible to know Him while living in this present evil world. Now Paul's knowledge of

SHADOWS OF REDEMPTION

the risen Saviour forms a link between the knowledge that was given to the apostles and the knowledge that may be ours. The bodily sight is not the main thing. Even that has not been denied to all men since the apostles. And the same words which properly describe bodily sight are used to describe that which we have now. "We see not yet all things put under Him…but we see Jesus, who was made a little lower than the angels for the suffering of death, crowned with glory and honor; that He by the grace of God should taste death for every man." You see he says, "We see Jesus." And again He bids us "run with patience the race that is set before us, looking unto Jesus." That is the only convincing evidence of the resurrection that we can have now.

I have often been struck and sometimes almost startled by that test propounded in the *Pilgrim's Progress,* to discover whether a man who professed to believe in Christ was a real Christian or not: "Ask him if he ever had Christ revealed to his soul from heaven." But I believe the test is a true one. He who has seen Jesus with the eye of faith as the One who was crucified and is risen; for He was always seen with the marks of death on His person to distinguish Him from all others who are in glory—"a Lamb as it had been slain," slain for you and for me. Everyone that has seen Him so, will have been satisfied that our Redeemer lives, "liveth and was dead," and "ever liveth," "able also to save them to the uttermost that come unto God by Him." And this revelation of the Lord Jesus to the soul is made by the Holy Spirit. For whenever the Holy Spirit presents a person to us, it is always the person

SEEN OF ME ALSO

of the Lord Jesus. "He shall receive of Mine and shall show it unto you."

At any time we may draw near boldly and ask confidently that we may have the revelation of the Lord Jesus to our souls from heaven. We may see Him and realize His presence, drawing nearer to Him than ever we have been before. Let us all ask today that this may be given us. "Lord, we wish to see Jesus." Surely He will not deny this petition. And thus the text will be true for each of us. "Last of all He was seen of me also." Not so soon as He might have been, if I had sought Him more earnestly. But "He was seen of me also, as of one born out of due time."

"Born out of due time." The expression is a remarkable one. It means literally an abortion. "He was seen of me also,"—His last born child, born "by the grace of God" And having seen Him, by the grace of God I shall be what I never could have been, but for His resurrection, and what I never was before.

CHAPTER TWELVE

THE PRINT OF THE NAILS

Then saith He to Thomas, Reach hither thy finger, and behold My hands; and reach hither thy hand, and thrust it into My side: and be not faithless, but believing. And Thomas answered and said unto Him, My Lord and my God.
JOHN 20:27-28

We have here the record of the special testimony to our Lord's resurrection which was given on the first Sunday after He rose from the dead. The story of the Apostle Thomas has often been made the subject of discourse, both in its bearing on his character, and in the lesson which it impresses upon ourselves. But there is another light in which we may regard it, which is perhaps the most important of all.

Thomas' doubting happened for the confirmation of our faith. And it will give us an opportunity to return to two points which we had to leave over from the previous chapter, *viz.,* (1) the doctrine of the resurrection and (2) the manner of our Lord's resurrection.

SHADOWS OF REDEMPTION

As to what made Thomas doubtful in this matter, it is not of so much consequence now. The two remarks of his which are recorded in the Gospel, "Lord, we know not whither Thou goest; and how can we know the way?" and "Let us also go, that we may die with Him," when our Lord proposed to go to Bethany to raise Lazarus—the only two recorded sayings of this apostle—both agree with the notion that he was a matter-of-fact kind of person, devotedly attached to his Master's person, ready to follow Him resolutely even to the death, but depending not much on his mind and imagination to help him; rather relying on what was actually before his eyes and within his grasp. There are many such persons in the world, and they can sympathize with one another. But they do not always meet with ready sympathy from clever persons, whose wits move more rapidly than theirs.

But the Gospel was not sent only for the quick. The greatest fool in Paradise knows more about things unseen than all the wisest in this present world. Moreover, the way of holiness is not especially for the wise. "The unclean shall not pass over it;" but "the wayfaring men, though fools, shall not err therein." One of the best of men said, "So foolish was I, and ignorant: I was as a beast before Thee." But "Thou shalt guide me with Thy counsel, and afterward receive me to glory."

But to return. For whatever reason, Thomas was so deeply convinced of our Lord's death, that he refused, without the most definite and tangible proofs, to allow the possibility of His resurrection. Every wound and mark on the slain body he well knew; the place of the

THE PRINT OF THE NAILS

print of the nails, and the greatness of the rent in His side, as large as an hand-breadth—he knew that well. He knew also that wounds like these are not to be healed in a day or two. And therefore when he heard of the resurrection, he not unnaturally demanded the most positive proofs that He who rose again was the same who had been slain.

The other disciples were not able to satisfy him. Although on Easter Day our Saviour had "showed them His hands and His feet," as Luke tells us, "and His side" also, as we are reminded by John, yet it does not appear that anyone had examined them very closely; perhaps from reverential awe and dread, perhaps also from that carelessness with which we often neglect to look closely at a thing before us, having satisfied ourselves by a glance that it is the thing we need. For had the apostles looked, as closely as Thomas proposed to look, at those marks of the nails and spear, they could surely have convinced him that they were not deceived.

His continued doubt more than half proves their imperfect observation. And indeed it is not everyone who observes so closely as to be able to swear positively under cross-examination that he saw what he says he saw. But matters of supreme importance demand thorough examination and absolute certainty. Here is a lesson, by the way, for rapid minds; not to be careless in their observations, lest too great speed should beget uncertainty.

Observe, also, the value to ourselves of what is recorded here. Had it only been written, as it is in the two places already referred to, that our Lord showed His hands and His feet and side, we should not have known in what condition those sacred wounds remained. It might have been matter of debate whether they were already healing. What is recorded here, suggests some interesting inquiries as to the nature of the resurrection body.

Let us inquire, however, what is the importance to the doctrine of the resurrection that these marks should remain. For, of course, they need not have remained. He who in one moment gave sight to the blind, made the maimed to be whole, restored withered hands, and gave health to leprous bodies—could He not have come forth from the grave, "all fair," not "the Lamb as it had been slain," but the " Lamb without blemish," even as He was in the fullest sense of the words "the Lamb...without spot?" Surely, the fact that He did not is peculiar, a thing belonging to Himself.

We do not expect the martyrs to carry eternally the marks of all they suffered. It is impossible. For in some instances we know that their enemies reduced the bodies of Christians to absolute dust, which they dispersed and scattered, as it were in open defiance of every conceivable theory of bodily resurrection. We do not think of glorified spirits as really entering into life "halt or maimed" in their resurrection bodies, although it might be better to enter into life so, than that the whole body should depart elsewhere. No, it cannot be that any of Christ's members should live mutilated throughout eternity. It is the "spirits of just men made perfect" who are gathered into the, city of God.

Why then, if the saints are to lose all marks of mortal suffering, why should it be otherwise with the "King of

THE PRINT OF THE NAILS

saints?" Why? Because these very marks are His own special glory, tokens of that which He did alone, Himself, and not another. Because, moreover, these marks are the only visible security that our debt is paid. What debtor would part with a receipt for payment that he had once obtained from his bitterest enemy. No! He would keep it forever in the safest place he knew.

These marks on our Saviour's person are the receipt and signature of the powers of darkness, for all our debts. They are Satan's handwriting accepted by Jehovah. They are the evidence that "He Himself bare our sins in His own body on the tree." By virtue of these marks He "entered in once into the holy place" in heaven, the true High Priest with the evidence of the death of Jehovah's great sin-offering—He "bare our sins." He presented in heaven the proofs that He had borne them. "Unto them that look for Him shall He appear the second time" in like manner as He appeared to His disciples, "without sin," but not without the tokens that He is the sin-bearer; "without sin unto salvation."

Let each of us ask the question, What more do I need to prove that Christ died for me than this; to see Him with the death wounds and yet living; the proof that He did bear sin upon His person, and on the same glorious person in every feature, the light and gladness that prove He is not bearing sin now?

The Jews of old sent the scape-goat far into the wilderness lest he should bring their sins back again. But what if he could have come back white as snow in proof that he had lost them?

Who that ever trusted the power of the Lord Jesus could see Him as one that liveth and was dead, and not believe forever in the forgiveness of sins? If I know that He did bear my sins, and the sin that He died for was none of His, what can I look for when I see Him without my sin, except salvation?

It appears, then, that when Thomas demanded to see and handle his Master's wounds, he was demanding, for one thing, the proof of our salvation. Whether he intended it or not, is not of so much importance. Enough that he did demand it, and the proof with which he was satisfied is now ours.

Another thing follows which is more mysterious. When Thomas saw the sight that he had asked for, he answered, "My Lord and my God!" If the doubts of this disciple are exceptional, his confession is also singular. No one else in all the Gospel addressed Jesus Christ as "God." Many said what implied it; many more believed it; but in all the four Gospels there is no one else who says exactly what Thomas said to his Master, that in one word He was God. And this he said upon receiving distinct proof that the Son of Man was risen.

I do not think the mind of Thomas reached this conclusion by any process of reasoning, though he had reason in our Saviour's expressed knowledge of his own thoughts and words. He did not stay to reason it out. He saw it, and he was the very man to grasp just what He saw. The words that burst from his lips were the irrepressible outcome and relief of the heart's overflow. He could not see, and yet refrain from worship. "Surely God

THE PRINT OF THE NAILS

is in Thee; and there is none else, there is no other God!"

To the same end must we come, if we ever reach it, by the very same path. To see Him as He is, and to be like Him, what is it but to know Him? And to know Him must be to worship Him. Then will the longings of our hearts be satisfied, those longings after Someone whom we can worship without fear of idolatry, One whom we can love without risk of disappointment, and adore without a whisper of suspicion that there is any possibility of change. That is one desire that will be satisfied with the personal presence of the Lord Jesus; and, let me add, that can never be satisfied with any thing or person short of Him. "The Deity of Christ," and "the forgiveness of sins" are two great doctrines thus confirmed and proved by the manifestation of the person of our risen Lord.

And now can we say anything as to the manner of the resurrection from what is before us here? "How are the dead raised up? And with what body do they come?" One point Thomas' doubts have cleared up beyond all question. The body that is raised in incorruption is in some sense the very same body that is laid in the grave. In saying this, we are safe. But in saying more than this, we enter upon the region of dispute and controversy, because it is the region of ignorance. "It doth not yet appear what we shall be." Identity is certain; we shall be the same persons, for Jesus Christ is the same. Recognition is certain; we shall know each other as they knew Him. Body, as well as spirit, is certain, for "spirit hath not flesh and bones, as ye see Me have."

But the precise relation between the body that shall

be, and the body that is now is not certain, and to our present understanding perhaps not possible to explain.

The illustration which our Lord used of His own case, and Paul of all cases, is that of the seed corn. "Except a corn of wheat fall into the ground and die, it abideth alone; but if it die, it bringeth forth much fruit." So spoke our Lord for the special comfort of the Gentiles on the last day of His public ministry. So too Paul: "That which thou sowest is not quickened except it die; and that which thou sowest, thou sowest not that body that shall be, but bare grain, it may chance of wheat, or of some other grain. But God giveth it a body as it hath pleased Him, and to every seed its own body" (1 Cor. 15:36-38).

Once more: There is a sowing in corruption, there is an awakening in incorruption. There is a sowing in dishonor, there is an awakening in glory; there is a sowing in weakness, there is an awakening in power; there is sown a body fitted to the being of a soul, there awakeneth a body fitted to the being of a spirit. For the first man Adam was made a living soul; the last Adam was made an enlivening or creating spirit (1 Cor. 15:42-45). Add to this that "flesh and blood can not inherit the kingdom of God," and that all who do inherit it "shall be changed," the "body of our humiliation" changed into "a glorious body," a mortal body quickened into that which can never die; and we have the greater part of what is said on the subject.

And in all this there are two sides, which are not really seen by all people. To some minds the resemblance and continuity of this life and the next are clearest. To others

THE PRINT OF THE NAILS

the difference seems so vast as to destroy all resemblance, as much as death seems absolutely to break the continuity. But both sides have their place in Scripture. Take the simple illustration of the corn of wheat. "That which thou sowest, thou sowest not that body that shall be, but bare grain." Yet it is as certain as anything in the world, that if you sow wheat, wheat and nothing else will come up. "Whatsoever a man soweth, that shall he also reap."

And that which we call death does not hold the same place as the death in the springing of the sown corn. We bury men's bodies after they are dead. We sow the seed corn because it is living, in order that it may die. If it were dead, we should not sow it, for dead seeds will not grow. A grain of corn may have lived for three thousand years in the hand of a mummy. It is sown at the end of that time, and in the ground it dies and brings forth much fruit. The thought suggested by this fact is, that the utter dissolution of our mortal bodies in the grave is the real preliminary; the death which precedes and makes resurrection possible. And indeed the resurrection body, the spiritual body, is so different from the mortal and natural body, that we may safely say the one cannot turn into the other without every single particle being changed.

It may well be, therefore, that those who reduced the bodies of the martyrs to absolute dust, did but fulfill more quickly that which was necessary to their resurrection. And even in the case of Him whom God raised up, who saw no corruption, we are sure that every portion of His body must have undergone a wondrous change, while its form remained unaltered. As "flesh and blood" it died, as "flesh and bones" it was raised up again. "Flesh and blood" it ceased to be, for "flesh and blood cannot inherit the kingdom of God."

Again, after its change, it seems to have been capable of instantaneous dissolution and reconstruction, so as to vanish here and appear there at pleasure, embodying the spirit wheresoever the spirit was to go. All this is quite beyond our understanding. But as life in the seed corn is necessary, before you can sow it with any hope that it will spring up again, so it is with ourselves. "If the spirit of Him that raised up Jesus from the dead dwell in you, He that raised up Christ from the dead shall also quicken your mortal bodies by (or because of) His Spirit that dwelleth in you." And even this does not explain that darker mystery of "the resurrection of the...unjust." But, for the most part, the life of the world to come is taught us by negatives.

"They shall hunger no more, neither thirst any more." Both "the belly and the meats" are to be done away with, and yet there may be "new wine" and "the marriage supper" in that world to come. "Blessed is he that shall eat bread in the kingdom of God!" Our Saviour Christ ate and drank with His disciples after He rose from the dead.

Again, "They neither marry, nor are given in marriage: neither can they die any more." No birth and no death are known among the angels. "And there shall be no night there;" and so no sleep and no weariness. What we are told of that life is very glorious. But when all is reported, we feel sure that the half is not told us, and the mind turns again and again to the simple words of a great writer, the author of the "Saint's Rest."

> *"My knowledge of that life is small,*
> *The eye of faith is dim;*
> *But 'tis enough that Christ knows all,*
> *And I shall be with Him."*

It is a great pleasure to speak and to meditate together in this life about the things concerning that kingdom. It was the design of our Creator to "make man in His image after His likeness, and to let them have dominion." In Jesus Christ that design is accomplished as regards His person. It has yet to be finished as regards His members. But He has counted the cost, and He "hath sufficient to finish it." "He shall build the temple of the Lord, and He shall bear the glory." It is our part to see that we do not hinder Him by our waywardness, negligence or unbelief.

Thus far, God helping me, I have preached to you "Jesus, and the resurrection." I cannot do better than conclude what has been said with the apostle's exhortation to us: "Therefore, my beloved brethren, be ye steadfast, unmoveable, always abounding in the work of the Lord, forasmuch as ye know that your labor is not in vain in the Lord."

CHAPTER THIRTEEN

FOLLOW ME

*Verily, verily, I say unto thee, When thou wast young,
thou girdedst thyself, and walkedst whither thou
wouldest: but when thou shalt be old, thou shalt stretch
forth thy hands, and another shalt gird thee, and carry
thee whither thou wouldest not. This spake He,
signifying by what death he should glorify God.
And when He had spoken this,
He saith unto him, Follow Me.*
JOHN 21:18-19

Of all human lives in the New Testament, perhaps there is not one that calls out our sympathy more than that of Peter. If there is one man of whom we can see that he was "subject to like-passions as we are," Peter is that man. And the words which we have just read give us a kind of vantage ground from which to view the life of Peter as a whole. We can see him as a young man, and we can see him as an old man; as a young disciple of Christ, and as an old disciple. And we see also the path of progress by which he grew in grace, until he had glorified

God, like his Master, by obedience, "even unto death"—and that being also death on a cross. Thus led the path of obedience to the call, "Follow thou Me."

Let me ask you to look at the life of Peter in these three points of view: first, as a young disciple, second, as an old disciple, and third, as a growing disciple. And let us study it with this purpose, that we may learn to follow him as he followed his master, Jesus Christ.

First, let us look at Peter as a young disciple. "Verily, verily, I say unto thee, When thou wast young, thou girdedst thyself, and walkedst whither thou wouldest." Perhaps you may think that these words are not applicable to a disciple of Christ at all, that they are spoken of his earlier life, before he was called to follow the Lord Jesus. Indeed it must have been so, because the words describe Peter's natural character—an impulsive, warmhearted, vigorous, impetuous man.

When he saw anything he would like to do, he girded up his loins, and went about it at once. And if any evil propensities or mischievous desires had taken hold of Peter's mind in his early days, he would have been a dangerous man. For he was just the man to lead others by his own energy of character into any kind of daring mischief. But however these words may apply to the beginning of his life before the Lord called him, a time of which the Gospel tells us nothing, we can see that after he became a disciple his natural disposition was not changed at once.

Peter was a wilful disciple, and an impetuous and energetic disciple, all the while the Lord Jesus went in and out with them upon earth. We can see it in the Gospel

FOLLOW ME

history again and again. We may almost say that there was a wilfulness even in his following Christ at all. We read of his saying on one occasion, "Lo, we have left all, and followed Thee." Not, "Thou hast called us, Thou hast chosen us and loved us, and drawn us after Thee." Not what Christ said, "Ye have not chosen Me, but I have chosen you." But *we* emphatically, "we" by our own act and deed, in the exercise of our free choice, "have forsaken all, and followed Thee. What shall we have therefore?"

On another occasion Peter would have turned his Master out of the path marked out for Him, into his own course. When He was speaking of the necessity of His sufferings, that He must go to Jerusalem and suffer many things, and be killed and be raised again, "Peter took Him, and began to rebuke Him, saying, Be it far from Thee, Lord: this shall not be unto Thee." And so strongly did the disciple urge this, that his Master was under the necessity of rebuking him sharply. "Get thee behind Me, Satan: thou art an offense unto Me."

Unless He had felt the force and effect of Peter's persuasions, He would never have spoken so sharply. Had it not been a real obstacle, He would not have thrust it aside so vigorously out of His path.

Peter's eagerness to speak on so many occasions is a token of his impulsive energy of character. Even when he knew not what to say, he would say something, if it were only to relieve his heart. At the bottom there is a good deal of self-will in a character like this. I do not say obstinacy, for Peter seems to have been peculiarly open to the influence of affection and kindness. If he was ready to express himself, he was equally ready to withdraw what was spoken, when he found he had said what he ought not. "Thou shalt never wash my feet," were his words to his Master on the last night before He died. But when the Master made it a personal question, "If I wash thee not, thou hast no part with Me," Peter cried out at once, "Lord, not my feet only, but also my hands and my head." And he would not only speak, but act to please his Master.

After the Saviour had gone into Peter's boat, and had sat for a while teaching, close by the shore, "when He had left speaking He said unto Simon, Launch out into the deep, and let down your nets for a draught." "Master," was the reply, "we have toiled all the night and have taken nothing; nevertheless at Thy word, I will let down the net." This was before they had left all to follow Jesus, before they had seen all those mighty works which He did in the presence of His disciples. Peter and Andrew were thoroughly tired of casting the net for nothing. And yet they were quite ready to cast it again at a single word from Christ. All this goes to show that Peter, like many another man, had a mixed character. He was a wilful impetuous disciple, but a disciple still. And, like many of the rest of us, I suspect he was not at all aware how wilful and impetuous he was.

Notice the way in which our Lord introduces this saying. "Verily, verily, I say unto thee, When thou wast young, thou girdedst thyself, and walkedst whither thou wouldest." I think it is not usual to find that solemn form of address, "Verily, verily, I say unto thee," prefixed to something which only concerns the nature of a man.

FOLLOW ME

Generally, when our Lord began this way, He went on to reveal some great truth about Himself, or His Father, or the way of salvation. "Verily, verily, I say unto thee, Except a man be born again, he cannot see the Kingdom of God." Or "He that believeth on Me hath everlasting life." Once indeed He does add something concerning man. "Verily, verily, I say unto you, that one of you shall betray Me." Still it is not often that a matter which concerns man only is introduced in this way. May we not say that our Lord need not thus have emphasized His saying to Peter, unless He was aware that the statement would not be easily received. We do not readily accept, or pay sufficient attention to, unfavorable descriptions of our own character. True they often stick in our memory, in spite of our dislike. But we like to ignore them and disregard them. We forget them if we can.

This statement of Peter's natural character was not to be lightly set aside or forgotten by him. "Verily, verily, I say unto thee," in thy younger days thou wast a wilful man! "When thou wast young, thou girdedst thyself, and walkedst whither thou wouldest." And even after the Lord had called him, the wilful man was for some time a wilful disciple too. But one day this would be altered.

Let us now look at Peter as an old disciple. "When thou shalt be old, thou shalt stretch forth thy hands, and another shall gird thee, and carry thee whither thou wouldest not." The first meaning of these words is, that when he was old, Peter would be crucified like his Master. "This spake He, signifying by what death he should glorify God."

Peter himself refers to it in his second epistle, 1:13-14: "Yea, I think it meet, as long as I am in this tabernacle, to stir you up by putting you in remembrance; knowing that shortly I must put off this my tabernacle, even as our Lord Jesus Christ hath showed me." And the tradition that so it came to pass has come down to us from early writers. Though whether it is true that by his own request the disciple was crucified with his head downwards, because he was not worthy to suffer as his Lord, I am disposed to doubt. I think that if it were so, we must call him a wilful disciple to the very end. Such a request would not have been a fulfillment of the Master's prophecy, but rather a deviation from the path of humble submission and obedience to God's appointment. I think that part of the tradition is a fantastic addition and embellishment, not coming from Apostolic times.

But, be that as it may, the thing on which our Lord lays most stress is not the literal crucifixion. He does not even mention the suffering, or the material cross. It is the submission of the will, the consent to be crucified at the will of another. That is the main point. Just as the actual girding and the literal walking are not the things rebuked in the former part of the description, but rather the inward uncontrolled self-will.

So again in the last part. It is not the actual girding and the literal carrying, or the precise form and position of the cross. Rather it is the glorifying God by patient submission to His will. "This spake He, signifying by what death he should glorify God." This was what the young disciple failed to do, though over and over again he professed himself ready to do it.

"Lord," he said, "I am ready to go with Thee, both to prison, and to death." And when our Saviour said, "Whither I go, thou canst not follow Me now; but thou shalt follow Me afterwards," the answer was, "Lord, why cannot I follow Thee now? I will lay down my life for Thy sake." When it came to the point, Simon Peter found it impossible. Not that his heart failed him. But the whole thing came in a different way from what he had expected. He thought that the disciples of the Master would, at the worst, have to stand back to back, and to defend themselves sword in hand against their adversaries. And if over-powered at last by numbers, they would either die together, or be taken together before the tribunal, and still stand side by side. But when the Lord Jesus deliberately severed Himself from His followers in the moment of betrayal, and gave Himself up, only asking permission for them to depart, He seemed to have abandoned the cause. How was it possible still to follow a leader who had now refused to lead? And so Peter followed Him afar off, and then denied Him.

His own strength and will failed him, because they could not teach him the ways and purposes of God. He would follow his Master, but he must follow Him in his own way. He could not follow the Master in that path of unknown and inconceivable self-sacrifice and love to man. What wonder? Which of us, my brethren, would have done better than Peter on that night of the Lord's betrayal? "Lord, is it I?"

But that which Peter failed to accomplish as a young

man in his own strength and by his own resolution, he was to do as an old man, by the strength of the Lord. "When thou shalt be old, thou shalt stretch forth thy hands, and another shall gird thee, and carry thee whither thou wouldest not." I think these words have a double meaning. Who was it that would gird Peter, and carry him where he would not go? Would it be the soldiers who arrested him, or led him from the prison to the place of execution, who nailed him to the cross and set him up to die? It may be that they are alluded to.

But I do not think that is all the meaning. More than one man was usually employed in the work of crucifixion. The crucifixion of our Saviour was assigned to four soldiers, who afterwards parted His garments and cast lots for His coat. But the girding and carrying of Peter is here represented as the work of one. It is not said, others shall gird thee, and carry thee, but "another shall gird thee, and carry thee." Another, that is, One other. And who was that one?

I think it was the One who said, "Even to your old age I am He, and even to hoar hairs will I carry you. I have made, and I will bear. Even I will carry and will deliver you." When Peter vowed that he would follow his Master in his own strength, his strength failed him. In his old age he followed Him alone, without any visible support or assistance, in the way that led to the cross, and never hesitated. For "the eternal God" was his "refuge, and underneath" him were "the everlasting arms."

And now we have looked at Peter as a young disciple, a self-willed man; and we have looked at him as an old

FOLLOW ME

disciple, obediently dying for the Lord whom he loved.

We have still to look at what lies between these two, and connects them together—as a growing disciple. What are the words that describe this—the longest and the most instructive part of his experience? The words that describe it are the two last words of the text. Our Lord first described him as he was in his younger days, and then as he would be in his older days. And when He had spoken this, He said unto him, "Follow Me." This was the rule by which Peter grew from a young disciple into an old disciple, from a self-willed disciple into an obedient disciple. It was by daily following the Master, who "suffered for us, leaving us an example, that we should follow His steps." Our Lord gave to Peter the privilege of following Him in a very uncommon way. He let him know, as we see by the text, that one day his life would end in being crucified.

He let him know of this end at the beginning of his ministry, before the Lord's ascension, before the day of Pentecost, before the door of faith was opened to Jews or Gentiles. All the years that Peter preached in Jerusalem, or Samaria, or Babylon, or wherever else he may have been sent, he went about as a man sentenced to be one day crucified.

It must have been a strange experience. Sometimes he may have thought little of it; sometimes almost forgotten it in the pressure and interest of his life and ministry. But he can never have parted with the knowledge. In moments of weariness and depression and hardship, sleeping and waking, in labor and at rest, he was always liable to this recollection, never safe from this picture—a cross prepared for him, and men taking hold of him and nailing him to it.

"Thou shalt stretch forth thy hands" to give up the use of them, never to have them free on earth again. It must have been a strange experience—to live on with this prospect, and in absolute certainty that, unless he again denied and forsook his dear Master, one day it must be no longer a prospect, or an imagination, but a painful and cruel reality.

It was a very wonderful bond between Peter and the Lord Jesus Christ. They were more like one another in this particular than any others who could be named on earth. Jesus Christ "for the joy that was set before Him endured the cross, despising the shame," not only for one day on Calvary, but all the days He looked forward to it upon earth. "He bearing His cross went forth" all the time of His ministry. And Peter went forth after Him, bearing his. He had the same kind of work to do as the Lord Jesus, preaching, teaching, and healing, feeding and keeping His lambs and His sheep, and the same end to look forward to through it all from first to last, fulfilling this saying, "If any man will come after Me, let him deny himself, and take up his cross daily, and follow Me." This was the path appointed for Peter to walk in, that he might "grow in grace."

It is worthwhile to notice that our Lord acknowledged Peter to have made some progress already, by a word that He employed in the text. As we read it, it runs thus: "When thou wast young, thou girdedst thyself." But real-

FOLLOW ME

ly the word for young means younger. "When thou wast younger, thou girdedst thyself." Take notice that the Lord Jesus watches every step and every degree of progress in a disciple. It was only a few days, or at most a few weeks, since Peter had denied Him. But the Lord Jesus had forgiven him, and asked and received the threefold profession of his love; and given him back his commission to "feed the flock of God."

He now gives him again his first commission, in the words, "Follow Me." Not as though Peter had never followed Him before. He *had* followed Him. And the growth and progress of the disciple was not all canceled even by his terrible fall. He was not so obedient as he would be; not an old disciple yet. But he was not so self-willed as he had been. He had been younger than he was at this day. "When thou wast younger, thou girdedst thyself, and walkedst whither thou wouldest." It is not all self-will now. Some day it will be obedience, even to the cross.

The words "Follow Me" recur very often in Peter's history. At his first call to leave the fishing at the sea of Galilee, we read that the Saviour said to him and to his brother, "Follow Me."

In a somewhat sharper form, it is the same lesson, when our Lord said to Peter, "Get thee behind Me." "What hast thou to do with peace" between Me and My adversary Satan? "Turn thee behind Me." Again at the last supper, "Lord, whither goest Thou?" "Whither I go thou canst not follow Me now, but thou shalt follow Me afterwards." Again in our text, and again when Peter asked about the beloved disciple, "Lord, and what of him?" "If I will that he tarry till I come, what is that to thee? Follow thou Me." And once more, on the night when Peter was asleep in Herod's prison waiting for trial on the morrow, the angel awoke him with these words, "Arise up quickly." "Gird thyself, and bind on thy sandals." "Cast thy garment about thee, and follow me." The last words the angel spoke to him were an echo of the Lord's commission, which was the motto of his life, "Follow thou Me." Not to the sword of Herod just at present, but in a further life of ministry, and by-and-by to the cross. But over and over again, in every different phase of life, it is the same lesson, "Follow Me."

I do not think many words of mine are needed to apply the lessons of the text. There is a message for those who are Christ's disciples, and a message for those who are not.

The message for Christ's disciples is in Peter's own words, "Grow in grace." "Grow in grace." And if you say, "How shall I grow in grace?" The answer is, "By treading in the Saviour's footsteps; not by girding and strengthening yourself, and walking where you will, but by denying self and bearing the cross daily, and following Him." Do you ask, "What cross?" The answer is, "Your own." Christ never left a disciple yet without a cross of some kind, seen or unseen. If you have not a cross, most likely you are no disciple. Something that interferes with self, and self-will and self-gratification; something that belongs to you, and lies before you, right in your path, if you attempt to live a life of obedience and captivity to the service of Jesus Christ that is your cross.

FOLLOW ME

That cross you must take up and carry daily, not in your own strength, not by your own resolution, but in the strength of the Lord who said, "I have made, and I will bear: even I will carry, and will deliver you!" Take it up and carry it, and learn to be obedient to that death, by which you may glorify God. It is not self you are to glorify; not man you are to glorify. You are not to make yourself glorious in the eyes of man, even by your Christianity. But be it crucified with Christ. And by that kind of death, grow in grace; until you have glorified God on the earth, by finishing the work that He has given you to do.

And to those who are not disciples, the text speaks in the words, "Thou girdedst thyself, and walkedst whither thou wouldest." Are there any of you who feel that this is just true of you? You need not necessarily be living immoral lives to make it true. Many people are kind because they like to be kind, and industrious because they like to be industrious, and outwardly religious because they like to be outwardly religious; and even self-denying because they like to be, and when they like to be. But yet they have never really submitted their understanding to God's Word, and their wills to the Lord Jesus Christ. They have never gone to Him to enter upon His secret service, saying, "Lord, what wilt Thou have me to do?" They have fished for themselves, and perhaps fished for others, like Simon Peter, but never once let down the net at the word of the Lord Jesus Christ.

Well, if you feel this is the case with you, let me ask you, Do you wish it to be so always? Has Peter's experience no attraction for you, even in spite of Peter's cross? Where is Peter now? Where has he been these nineteen hundred years past? With Christ in glory. In Paradise, amid the things that "eye hath not seen, nor ear heard, neither have entered into the heart of man, the things which God hath prepared for them that love Him." Do you think Peter regrets the cross, or the days in which he went forward to meet it, obeying his Master's order, "Follow Me"?

Do those days of labor, and anticipation of sorrow, seem dark and long at this distance? Or has the "far more exceeding and eternal weight of glory" outweighed them, obliterated them, and recompensed them, so that they are "no more remembered, neither come into mind"? If it was "joy unspeakable and full of glory" to rejoice in an unseen Saviour, what must it be to see Him face to face? Oh, is it not worthwhile even to be crucified, if you may be sure of the eternal love and fellowship of the Lord Jesus Christ?

How miserable, if when we see Him, as "every eye shall see Him, and they also which pierced Him," He has nothing to say to us but, "Thou hast girded thyself, and walked whither thou wouldest all thy life long, and thou shalt not walk with Me now. Depart, and go where thou canst depart unto the everlasting fire, to be with the devil and his angels." O God forgive us, and be merciful to us! God forbid that we should ever think of choosing our own will and our own way for this life, instead of treading in the steps of Him who "bare our sins in His own body on the tree."

FOLLOW ME

"Forasmuch then as Christ hath suffered for us in the flesh, arm yourselves likewise with the same mind: for he that hath suffered in the flesh hath ceased from sin; that he no longer should live the rest of his time in the flesh to the lusts of men, but to the will of God." If you desire to follow in the steps of the Saviour, come to Him, and fall down on your knees before Him, as did Peter, saying, "I am a sinful man, O Lord, and if Thou wash me not I can have no part with Thee. Lord, wash me, and make me clean. Lord, not my feet only, but also my hands and my head. Wash me throughly from mine iniquity, and cleanse me from my sin. And teach me to do Thy will and to follow Thee. Let Thy loving spirit lead me into the land of uprightness, and make me Thy faithful follower and servant unto my life's end."

SCRIPTURE INDEX

GENESIS		LEVITICUS		9:18-19	163
1:26	62, 76, 151	2	12	2 CHRONICLES	
2:17	60	2:1	12	24:22	57
3:4	60, 68	DEUTERONOMY		JOB	
3:6	98	4:29	54	1:10	82
3:8	611	4:32	117	11:12	113
3:14-15	61-62	6:16	89-90	42:5-6	129
3:16-19	62	25:18	102	PSALM	
3:18	67	33:27	160	36:9	31
5:1-2	63-64	33:29	108	40:6	17
12:1	50	JOSHUA		40:6-8	13
15:13	51	24:32	52	45:2	34
16:7	31	JUDGES		50:21	23
18	33	2:1-2	32	51:2	167
32:24-32	33	2:4	32	73:22	142
48:15-16	33	6	33	73:24	142
EXODUS		7:2	103	85:7	115
3:12	51	16:12	102	90:17	x
4:22	52	1 KINGS		91:11-12	87-88
7:9	99	10:2	112	115:1	104
13:13	113	19:9-18	33	118:25	105
17:7	89-90	2 KINGS		119:94	114
19:4	53	2:11	112	119:176	114-115
33:11	33	4	85	126:1-2	44

130:8	117	Zechariah		22:42	106
143:10	167	6:13	20, 151	23:13-33	106
Proverbs		9:9	45, 105-115	23:38	106
12:28	69	12:10	130	23:38-39	39
24:11-12	127	Malachi		24:2	47
Song of Songs		3:1	30, 34	24:3	106
4:7	144			25:31	107
Isaiah		Matthew		25:32	107
33:14	111	1:21	99	26:22	124, 159
33:17	34	4:1	81-91	26:53-54	79
33:24	111	4:3	83, 94	27:42	109
35:8	142	4:4	84	27:63	107
45:14	147	4:5	93	28:2	133
46:4	160, 165	4:5-6	86	28:4	133
57:15	55	4:6	94	28:20	28
65:17	166	4:7	89	Mark	
66:1-2	55	4:8-10	93-104	1:13	74, 82
Jeremiah		4:10	94, 96	6:45-5:1	33
2:24	114	5:43	56	7:24-30	33
13:23	101	6:13	91	11:13	67
17:9	110	9:9	33	15:26	97
50:44	83	11:19	119	15:38	19
Daniel		11:20	106	Luke	
2:35	41	11:28-29	69	3:4	73
2:44	40	14:12	28	4:2	82
3	33	16:22	155	4:5	94
3:1	54	16:23	155, 163	4:9	86-87, 94
6	33	17:21	91	4:10-11	86-87
9:26	121	18:8	144	4:13	74
Amos		19:27	155	4:27	85
5:27	54	21:2	113	5:4-5	156
Micah		21:5	108	5:8	167
5:5	45	21:10	113	9:23	162
Zephaniah		21:42	40	10:24	75
3:14-17	114	21:44	40	10:28	155

SCRIPTURE INDEX

11:51	57	2:21	48	20:27-28	141-151
14:15	150	3:3	157	21:3-14	33
14:28	151	3:6	101-102	21:17	35
14:31	81	3:14-16	63	21:18-19	153-167
16:9	68	3:29	34	21:21	163
18:1-8	41-45	4:7	31	21:22	154, 164
19:10	31, 115	4:21	48	21:23	68
19:30	113	6:12	98	21:25	76
20:35-36	150	6:37	85	Acts	
20:38	90	6:47	157	2:24	66
21:28	38	7:46	32	4:10-12	40
22:28	74-75	8:29	90	6:8-8:2	47-58
22:31	77	8:48	59	6:14	47-58
22:33	159	8:51	59-70	7:1	49
22:42	19, 66	10:27-28	70	7:2	50
22:44	67	11:16	142	7:5	50
22:46	77	11:26	67-68	7:6-7	51
22:53	77	12:15	114	7:9	51
23:34	56	12:21	139	7:13	39
23:39	109	12:24	148	7:15-16	52
23:41	122	13:8-9	156, 167	7:36	53
24:13-27	34	13:13	104	7:43	54
24:16	135	13:21	124, 157	7:44	55
24:18	117-130	13:36	159, 163	7:46-47	55
24:21	108	13:37	159	7:48	48, 55
24:25	121	14:5	142	7:49-50	55
24:34	135	14:30	74	7:57	49
24:39	147, 149	15:16	66, 155	7:59	56-57
24:40	143	16:14	36, 139	7:60	56-57
John		16:21-22	65	9:6	165
1:1	61	17:4	16	10:41	133
1:18	30	19:9	79	12:7-8	164
1:23	73	19:11	124	13:30	133
1:29	73	19:17	162	17:18	151
1:46	73	20:20	143	22:11	137

24:15	150	15:36-38	148	2:10	109
25:11	56	15:42-45	148	2:14	149
26:13	137	15:47	67	2:18	100
ROMANS		15:50	148, 150	4:14	80
4:25	136	15:52	134, 148	4:15	71-80, 81, 99-100
5:6	111	15:58	151		
5:8	110	2 CORINTHIANS		4:16	80
5:10	130	4:10	103	5:2-3	19
6:4	111	4:17	166	5:7	18, 109
6:6	102	5:17	101	5:9	59, 109
6:9	67	5:21	102	7:25	109, 138
7:4	67	6:16	70	7:27	21
7:24	102	12:2	86-87	8:3	11-23
8:11	150	GALATIANS		8:4	19
11:25-26	38-39	4:19	65	9:12	16, 109, 145
12:21	35	4:25	51		
14:8	69	6:7	149	9:14	19
15:4	37	EPHESIANS		9:24	20
1 CORINTHIANS		2:2	94	9:25	21
2:8	97	3:20	25	9:26	16
2:9	166	5:30	67	9:28	145
6:13	150	PHILIPPIANS		10:5	18
10:13	81	2:8	154	10:5-7	13
11:3	64	3:21	148	10:9	13
15:3	118	COLOSSIANS		10:10	17
15:4-5	132, 136	1:14	119, 147	10:12	11, 18
15:5-8	132, 134	1:24	65, 68	10:14	17
15:6	27	3:1	20	10:26	18
15:8	131-139	3:16-17	70	11:9	50
15:10	139	1 THESSALONIANS		11:10	51
15:14	136	4:14	68	12:1	29
15:17	136, 149	HEBREWS		12:1-2	138
15:18	136	1:3	11	12:2	162
15:25	20	2:8-9	138	12:4	80
15:35	147	2:9	72	12:23	144

SCRIPTURE INDEX

13:1	28	2:24	145, 166	2:17	104
13:2	28	3:18	112	3:16	35
13:3	28	4:1-2	167	3:18	80
13:4-5	28-29	5:2	163	3:19	35
13:7	26, 27, 29	5:4	69	3:20	23
13:8	25-36	2 PETER		3:21	104
13:9	28-29	1:13-14	158	3:22	23
13:12	16	3:18	162, 164	4:11	95
13:16-18	29	1 JOHN		5:6	16, 138, 144
13:20-21	29	2:1	109, 112	6:2	112-113
JAMES		2:2	112	6:9	57
1:13	82	2:16-17	98	6:10	57
4:14	69	2:28	36	7:14	64-65
5:4	45	3:2	147	7:16	31, 150
5:7	37-45	3:16	122	7:17	31
5:17	153	REVELATION		11:15	41
1 PETER		1:5	108, 119	15:3	144
1:4	69, 111	1:5-6	130	19:9	150
1:8	27, 166	1:7	166	22:5	150
1:19	144	1:18	138		
2:21	161	2:7	104